Teacher to Teacher Mentality

Teacher to Teacher Mentality

Purposeful Practice in Teacher Education

Edited by Caroline M. Crawford
and Sandra L. Hardy

ROWMAN & LITTLEFIELD
Lanham • Boulder • New York • London

Published by Rowman & Littlefield
A wholly owned subsidiary of The Rowman & Littlefield Publishing Group, Inc.
4501 Forbes Boulevard, Suite 200, Lanham, Maryland 20706
www.rowman.com

Unit A, Whitacre Mews, 26–34 Stannary Street, London SE11 4AB

Copyright © 2017 by Caroline M. Crawford and Sandra L. Hardy

All rights reserved. No part of this book may be reproduced in any form or by any electronic or mechanical means, including information storage and retrieval systems, without written permission from the publisher, except by a reviewer who may quote passages in a review.

British Library Cataloguing in Publication Information Available

Library of Congress Cataloging-in-Publication Data Is Available

ISBN 978-1-4758-3923-4 (cloth: alk. paper)
ISBN 978-1-4758-3924-1 (pbk: alk. paper)
ISBN 978-1-4758-3925-8 (electronic)

∞™ The paper used in this publication meets the minimum requirements of American National Standard for Information Sciences—Permanence of Paper for Printed Library Materials, ANSI/NISO Z39.48–1992.

Printed in the United States of America

Contents

Foreword		vii
Nancy P. Gallavan		
Preface		xi
Acknowledgments		xv
Editors' Note		xix
Caroline M. Crawford and Sandra L. Hardy		
Introduction		xxi
Caroline M. Crawford and Sandra L. Hardy		
Overview and Framework		xxv
Caroline M. Crawford and Sandra L. Hardy		
1	Learning Communities in Practice and Induction: Implications for Professional Development Organizations *Sandra L. Hardy*	1
2	Qualities of Effective Teacher Leaders *Meagan Musselman, Lynn Gannon Patterson, and Greg Gierhart*	35
3	As the Moments Unfold: Developing Dispositions in Student Teacher–Mentor Teacher Relationships *Janine S. Davis and Victoria B. Fantozzi*	51
4	An Enhanced Role for Classroom Teachers During Student Teaching: Effective Collaboration Within a Professional Learning Community *Billi L. Bromer*	69

5	Critical Understandings of Classroom Teachers as Associated Teacher Educators on Learning in Landscapes of Practice: A Case Study Approach *Sandra L. Hardy and Caroline M. Crawford*	85
	Afterword *Caroline M. Crawford and Sandra L. Hardy*	109
	References	113
	About the Editors	115
	About the Contributors	117

Foreword

Serving as the president of the Association of Teacher Educators (ATE) includes the privilege of appointing one or two Commissions to guide the association with topics and issues in education. This privilege is accompanied with the responsibility of identifying particular areas of importance and/or concern as well as inviting interested members to participate on the Commissions. Commissions allow ATE members to meet regularly to discuss research and practices followed by opportunities to disseminate presentations and publications. By delving into multiple perspectives associated with a particular area and deliberating the impact on teacher education, Commission members help inform and support both the actions of ATE and contribute to the research literature grounding teacher education.

The ATE Commission on Classroom Teachers as Associated Teacher Educators is one Commission that I joyously appointed in 2013 as I began my ATE presidency. My vision for this Commission was to consider the research and resources available to classroom teachers and that ATE can promote combined with the technological avenues that ATE can establish to strengthen the educational preparation of our vital partners in teacher education found in the field.

I greatly value the expertise of classroom teachers, the energies they dedicate to their learners, and the experiences they provide in the preparation of classroom teachers; appointing this Commission allowed me to empower and equip teacher educators both at universities and in classrooms. Establishing this Commission sparked the conversations to revisit the origin of ATE and the contributions to education given that ATE began in 1920 as the National Association of Directors of Supervised Student Teaching,

I believe that teacher education involves the aligned messages, modeling, methods, and mentoring from two significant sources: (1) expert university instructors and well-developed courses in teacher education and (2) experienced P-12 teachers and classrooms in a variety of content subject areas, educational settings, and diverse communities. Sound research and accrediting agencies have long rationalized that teacher preparation requires strong partnerships between university instructors and classroom teachers.

My aim was to select a group of ATE members ascribing to this belief. In addition, my own career resonates the reciprocity shared between the university and the classroom; I have evolved from an undergraduate education candidate who prepared to be a classroom teacher, an intern in the classroom, a novice teacher, a graduate student teacher leader, a classroom intern mentor, and a doctoral candidate to a teacher educator, an intern supervisor, and a teacher educator preparing future doctoral teacher educators. Therefore, appointing this ATE Commission was a natural reflection of my life's work and meaningful decision for the ATE.

For many years, educators have faced an unresolved dilemma in teacher preparation. Many teacher preparation personnel and programs grapple with the dynamics involved in their partnerships with school administrators and classroom teachers. Likewise, many school administrators and classroom teachers wrestle with the expectations in their partnerships with universities and interns. Everyone agrees that new classroom teachers must be prepared by qualified teacher educators for ever-changing educational contexts. However, only through a seamless partnership specifying the purposes of each participant in the preparation of teachers will the intern, P-12 learners, classroom teachers, educational systems, and teacher preparation benefit.

As an educator who has evolved from a classroom teacher to a university instructor, I am fully aware of one overarching concern. Frequently, when classroom teachers are asked to mentor a university teacher preparation intern, the classroom teachers do not view themselves as teacher educators, nor do they approach mentoring as an opportunity contributing to their personal growth, professional development, and pedagogical expertise. Too often, classroom teachers respond to the request to mentor interns as another task consuming their time, energy, and sometimes, their money. Revisiting the purposes and practices of a seamless partnership between the teacher preparation program and the P-12 school poses five specific benefits for the classroom teacher that may influence teacher preparation processes and outcomes.

BENEFIT ONE

While mentoring a university teacher preparation intern, the classroom teacher has the rare opportunity to view individual practices through the eyes of another professional in a nonthreatening environment. Few professions offer this type of chance to reflect critically on one's own practices then to modify and advance practices appropriately. Most teachers think about improving their practices as if someone were watching; mentoring an intern transforms thoughts into authentic outcomes.

BENEFIT TWO

While transforming thoughts into authentic actions, the classroom teacher can develop mechanisms to enhance teacher self-efficacy. Most classroom teachers who are asked to mentor an intern demonstrate proficiencies to guide and support an apprentice. These proficiencies indicate that the classroom teacher has developed the confidence and competence to affect and promote student learning with comfort and care for the learner and the teacher. The opportunity to mentor an intern encompasses the optimal professional development.

BENEFIT THREE

While optimizing professional development, the classroom teacher also has the opportunity to transform personal growth and pedagogical expertise. As a mentor, the classroom teacher may realize the individual benefits from the passage of time and the discoveries from experience. These insights provide the intern with the most valuable perceptions that the intern will glean and take into her or his own career. The keen classroom teacher recognizes these unique and astute moments for one generation to shape future generations.

BENEFIT FOUR

While shaping future generations, the classroom teacher not only gains in pedagogical expertise but also increases acumen into adragogical practices. University interns are adults aspiring to become classroom teachers. Although the classroom teacher mentor and the university intern are focused on advancing their pedagogical expertise to increase the engagement and achievement of their students, the relationship between the mentor and the intern centers on andragogical practices related to the teaching, learning, and schooling of adults.

Knowles (1980, 1984) identified five characteristics of andragogy essential for the education of adults: (a) adults are moving from dependency to self-directedness; (b) experiences accumulate into resourcefulness; (c) readiness to learn is oriented as developmental tasks of social roles; (d) perspectives change from postponed or future use to immediate application accompanied with a shift from subject centeredness to problem centeredness; and (e) motivation becomes internal rather external.

BENEFIT FIVE

Consequently, while experiencing the transformation of the intern, the classroom teacher is also experiencing transformation in ways that benefit the teacher, the students, the school, and the community. Many classroom teachers who mentor interns discover new horizons in education prompting them to pursue additional endorsements, advanced degrees, and new career choices such as university teacher educators. Unlike the teaching, learning, and schooling associated with P-12 students, mentoring interns offers classroom teachers with new, perhaps endless, possibilities. I certainly can attest that this series of transformations influenced my career.

CONCLUDING THOUGHTS

I am excited that the members of the ATE Commission on Classroom Teachers as Associated Teacher Educators have authored this text. Shepherded by the Commission Text co-chairs, Caroline M. Crawford and Sandra L. Hardy have assembled a fascinating collection of outstanding research and principles applicable to teacher preparation, professional development, and learning communities. These insightful chapters provide well-developed purposes and practices contributing to the roles, responsibilities, and rigor of classroom teachers who mentor interns in their transformation as teacher educators and partners in the preparation of teachers. I greatly appreciate the dedication of this text's coeditors and all of the authors who have contributed to its success.

—**Nancy P. Gallavan**,
Association of Teacher Educators President, 2013–2014

REFERENCES

Knowles, M. (1980). *The modern practice of adult education: From pedagogy to andragogy*. Wilton, CN: Association Press.
Knowles, M. (1984). *Andragogy in action*. San Francisco, CA: Jossey-Bass.

Preface

Teacher to teacher mentality reflects purposeful practice of applied professional standards and dispositions that are evident within real-world classroom engagement. Purposeful practice extends to working closely with teachers, administrators, and university-based instructors. Such purposeful practice promotes the preparation and development of classroom teachers as associated teacher educators.

The classroom teacher as associated teacher educator holds a significant talent pool that is necessary and appropriate toward supporting the teacher candidate: a level of subject matter expertise; an understanding of the curricular design and student learner cognitive needs as well as developmental understandings; instructional prowess within the current K-12 classroom experiential needs; and dispositional understandings and the ability to assess the teacher candidates within a real-world environment, alongside the university instructor personnel. The ability to embrace K-12 classroom teaching while training teacher candidates, mentoring novice teachers, or supporting experienced colleagues is a role that deserves further recognition.

The Association of Teacher Educators' (ATE) Commission on Classroom Teachers as Associated Teacher Educators is a professional community focusing upon the professional development needs of classroom teachers as associated teacher educators. A classroom teacher who takes on the role of an *associated teacher educator* is a quality professional who focuses additional time, effort, and subject matter expertise upon supporting and training preservice teacher candidates, and novice teachers, as well as experienced colleagues within the field-based classroom environment and across settings.

The Commission on Classroom Teachers as Associated Teacher Educators brings forth three distinct yet related texts: The first text, *Redefining Teacher Preparation: Learning From Experience in Educator Development,* highlights applications and reflections of Association of Teacher Educator (ATE) Standards and offers conceptual frameworks and contextual realities in connections to classroom educators at all stages of their career.

The second text, *Dynamic Principles of Professional Development: Essential Elements of Effective Teacher Preparation,* focuses upon differentiated elements toward inquiry and the reflectivity of practitioners as dynamic components of professional development.

The third text, *Teacher to Teacher Mentality: Purposeful Practice in Teacher Education,* focuses upon professional discourse that revolves around induction efforts resulting from educators working together to inform one another's practice.

Association of Teacher Educators (ATE) promotes advocacy, equity, leadership, and professionalism for classroom teachers as associated teacher educators in all settings and supports quality education and collegial support for all learners at all levels. An understanding of the Association of Teacher Educators' (ATE) Commission on Classroom Teachers as Associated Teacher Educators may be framed through the innovative efforts of Dr. Nancy Gallavan, ATE past president, as her insightful vast understandings of teacher education transformations led to the realization of this Commission.

The Association of Teacher Educators' (ATE) Commission on Classroom Teachers as Associated Teacher Educators (active from 2013 through 2016) has been productively engaged in enriching discussions and cutting-edge efforts, not only through a theoretical and research focus, but also through the attainment of classroom teacher input. The Commission's overall efforts, vision, and mission are reflected through these three texts as representation of the current state of classroom teachers as associated teacher educators while promoting avenues for future developments in this regard.

COMMISSION VISION

The Association of Teacher Educators' (ATE) Commission on Classroom Teachers as Associated Teacher Educators promotes advocacy, equity, leadership, and professionalism for classroom teachers as associated teacher educators in all settings and supports quality education and collegial support for all learners at all levels and contexts.

COMMISSION MISSION

The Association of Teacher Educators' (ATE) Commission on Classroom Teachers as Associated Teacher Educators advocates quality teacher education through exemplary collaborative efforts and collegial support that reflect the inherent importance of classroom teachers as associated teacher educators.

As ATE past president Nancy Gallavan (2013–2014) has described the charge of the Association of Teacher Educators' (ATE) Commission on Classroom Teachers as Associated Teacher Educators to include the consideration of the research and resources available to classroom teachers. Further the Commission's mission recognizes that ATE promotes, combined with the technological avenues, the ATE establishment of informative and supportive vital educational preparation of partners in the field.

With the esteemed group of Commission colleagues that Dr. Gallavan coalesced, the Commission brings forward meaningful ideas for projects, research endeavors, publication efforts, as well as considerations toward enhancing grant funded areas of focus. The Commission also paves pathways toward further establishing ATE as a primary resource through which to obtain high-quality professional development opportunities, with special emphasis upon classroom teachers as associated teacher educators to mentor and guide teacher candidates, novice classroom teachers, and colleagues.

Acknowledgments

CAROLINE M. CRAWFORD

There are so many colleagues who have been involved in the success of this text. I would like to first acknowledge the Association of Teacher Educators (ATE) as a truly extraordinary professional organization. The professionals within this organization live, breathe, and forever journey through strengthening the profession of teacher education. Through the ATE, I have been honored to meet, work with, and forever have been impacted by truly extraordinary teacher educators, who have supported my understandings within the field as well as developed a sense of a welcoming family among our ATE membership.

I would like to begin this discussion through an acknowledgment of my deep respect and collegial admiration for Dr. Nancy P. Gallavan. Her trust and belief in my abilities led toward this opportunity to chair the Association of Teacher Educators' (ATE) Commission on Classroom Teachers as Associated Teacher Educators that occurred from 2013 through 2016. These 3 years were an amazing experience and quite a learning journey, for which I will always be grateful.

I would also like to bring forward my appreciation for our many colleagues who engaged in our Commission on Classroom Teachers as Associated Teacher Educators as committee members who engaged in our mission quite selflessly. Each committee member brought forward their own professional strengths, qualities, and pleasant creativity as we progressed forward toward realizing our Commission successes. The strength of understanding and depth of respect for professional classroom teacher colleagues were inherent in each undertaking and realized within each of the Commission successes.

I would like to state my respect for the amazing talents that each of our Committee Member colleagues brought forward toward supporting our mission, as well as the thoughtful efforts recognized within each demanding undertaking. The Commission membership has every reason to reflect a level of accomplishment throughout our Commission experience, as our years together have not only strengthened our professional understandings but also added fundamental and essential work to the professional knowledge base.

I would also like to acknowledge and deeply thank Dr. Sandra L. Hardy for being such an integral part of our text as an integral coeditor, as well as fundamentally important in our Commission's success. Thank you for always being professional, amazingly supportive, always going so far above and beyond all of my hopes for support, and for reflecting your true self as a proficient, skilled, knowledgeable, generous, kind, and caring professional. This text would not have been realized without your depth of engagement throughout our journey.

A truly amazing faculty advisor, mentor, and ultimate teacher educator is a rare gem of a professional. This describes Dr. Allen R. Warner, professor emeritus, from the University of Houston in Houston, Texas, USA. I still find it difficult to describe the deeply professional and personal impact that I have been honored to experience as I reflect upon my doctoral studies, tenure-track faculty years and as a tenured faculty member within the higher education university environment. Dr. Warner must be acknowledged as a true academic scholar and a true teacher educator.

Throughout my doctoral studies, Dr. Warner represented the faculty advisor guidance, patience, and benevolent oversight that developed my true understanding of the profession as one worthy of the highest esteem. Even after so many hours, days, months, and years of sacrificing his own time and effort toward supporting his students, the only request has been to *pass it forward* and impact others as profoundly as Dr. Warner impacted my own professional understanding and career path. I imagine that Dr. Warner may never know the true depth and breadth of his impact upon his students and colleagues, but I want to ensure this small acknowledgment highlights his truly significant career.

Finally, I would like to acknowledge the quality of university students with whom I have been honored to work. The undergraduate and graduate students with whom I have worked over the decades are exemplary examples of what I consider to be the best and the brightest within academia.

Students with whom I have been honored to work come from innumerable realms, including PreK-12 education systems as classroom teachers and professional staff, business and industry, medical education, higher education, and so many associated venues within which teaching, training, and instructional design quality support the vision and mission of the organizations.

I learn just as much from my learner colleagues as what I share, and for this reinvigorating energy, creativity, innovation, and sense of community, I am forever grateful.

SANDRA L. HARDY

The completion of the Commission on Classroom Teachers as Associated Teacher Educators three texts—*Redefining Teacher Preparation: Learning From Experience in Educator Development; Dynamic Principles of Professional Development: Essential Elements of Effective Teacher Preparation; Teacher to Teacher Mentality: Purposeful Practice in Teacher Education*—was made possible because of the diligent work ethic and dedication of so many individuals. I would like first and foremost to express immense gratitude to the Association of Teacher Educators (ATE) for bringing together a multitude of educators at all levels of the spectrum from preservice teachers through college deans.

ATE supports on so many levels the professional development of teachers, administrators, and teacher educators at all stages of their career and provides the opportunity to come together and learn from one another on a local, national, and international scale. ATE is also an organization that fosters teacher leadership. It is through the dynamic leadership and keen insight of former ATE president, Dr. Nancy P. Gallavan that our Commission on Classroom Teachers as Associated Teacher Educators came to fruition. Thank you, Dr. Nancy P. Gallavan.

Our commission was further enriched by the exemplary leadership of Dr. Caroline M. Crawford as commission chair. Dr. Crawford, also the coeditor of the afore mentioned books, time and again went far above and beyond the duties of chairing the commission to ensure that each member had ample opportunities to both express their ideas and unleash their full potential as commission members, members of the teaching profession and learning communities.

Further, Dr. Caroline M. Crawford served as an amazing mentor to me throughout the entire editing process. With Dr. Caroline M. Crawford's steadfast leadership we rose time and again above and beyond tremendous challenges and recognized the importance of details to keep the texts moving forward. For all this and so much more, I am deeply thankful to Dr. Caroline. M. Crawford.

I pause at this juncture to recognize two outstanding teacher educators who influence and serve the education community in an exemplary fashion, Dr. D. John McIntyre and Dr. Christie McIntyre. Dr. D. John McIntyre, former ATE president, was also the chair of my doctoral committee as well as one of my teacher educators. Dr. D. John McIntyre serves as a shining example of an outstanding teacher educator, administrator, researcher, author, and editor. Dr. McIntyre provides encouragement and guidance to doctoral students and brings the long arduous journey of their dissertation to a successful defense.

Dr. Christie McIntyre, current ATE president for the Illinois State chapter, early childhood teacher educator, researcher, and role model for teacher educators, also contributes to doctoral students educational programs and committees, and serves the education communities in so many ways in her support to teachers, students, and as a model to teacher educators both in the university classroom and in the field as well as in to the learning communities. Thank you, Dr. D. John McIntyre and Dr. Christie McIntyre.

I would also like to express my sincere gratitude to each and every individual who contributed their work to the content of our commission's written works. Without their giving selflessly of their professional knowledge, skills, abilities, and time the completion of these endeavors would not have been possible. Each author, as well as each assistant and associate reviewer, is a shining example of the education profession in their area of expertise. The culmination of these many individual professional teacher educators brought forth collectively the fruition of our Commission's efforts that will further serve to enrich the teaching profession and bring insight and support to many teachers across the teaching continuum for years to come. Thank you to all those teachers who made our mission a reality.

In closing, I embrace this opportunity to extend a heartfelt expression of gratitude to all of the truly dedicated professional educators who work tirelessly with compassion to make a difference in the life of so many individual teachers and learners in more ways than they may ever know. I further acknowledge with appreciation the multitude of learning communities who provide the support networks and link resources for teachers as learners and teacher educators to collaboratively improve their practice as they progress with renewal in all stages of professional development. Some of these educators participated in the completion of these texts, and some are a part of the research that is written about in the chapters.

Many are the educators who will find knowledge and support through the reading, discussion, and application of the content in the three texts brought forth by the Commission of Classroom Teachers as Associated Teacher Educators on behalf of the Association of Teacher Educators.

Editors' Note

Caroline M. Crawford and Sandra L. Hardy

The editors would like to thank the hard work and extensive efforts of their reviewers.

EDITORIAL ADVISORY BOARD OF REVIEWERS

Associate Reviewers: Book Chapter Manuscript Reviewers

The significant impact of the chapters' associate reviewers was truly appreciated. Dr. Billi Bromer, Dr. Caroline M. Crawford, Dr. Nancy Gallavan, Dr. Sandra L. Hardy, and Dr. Jennifer Young extended their professional time, effort and expertise toward carefully reviewing and offering detailed feedback throughout the second round of book chapter double-blind reviews. The editors would like to extend their heartfelt appreciation for these professionals who were able to extend themselves beyond the bounds of normal expectations.

Assistant Reviewers: Book Chapter Proposal Reviewers

The initial double-blind peer-review efforts of the submitted proposals for this text's journey were extensions of professional creativity and innovation and were innumerable. The professional efforts and expertise of their assistant reviewers brought forward the strengths of each proposal, for which Dr. Crawford and Dr. Hardy would like to state their deep appreciation to Dr. Billi Bromer, Dr. Lynda Cavazos, Dr. Caroline M. Crawford, Dr. Nancy Gallavan, Dr. Sandra L. Hardy, and Dr. Lisa Huelskamp.

They were integrally important, very much valued, respected, and each professional is highly esteemed for their depth of review effort. The high quality and impact of this text would not have been realized, without the assistant reviewer's initial strength of effort. For this, Dr. Crawford and Dr. Hardy offer significant thanks.

Introduction

Caroline M. Crawford and Sandra L. Hardy

Teacher to teacher mentality is the product of purposeful practice as educators serve to inform one another's preparation and development. Further, such mentality transcends boundaries to reach all levels of education and across contexts with cutting-edge research and applications that promote the classroom teacher as associated teacher educator in the process. Therefore, this text is meant as a reflection of the current *state of the profession* and future research and development prospects pertaining to the concept of classroom teachers as associated teacher educators who through teacher to teacher mentality inform purposeful practice.

Thus, this text serves also as a tool for promoting professional discourse concerning the classroom teachers as associated teacher educators in this regard. This is such an important discussion to be had, and yet only recently has the teacher education profession more fully realized, acknowledged, and emphasized the integral impact of teacher to teacher mentality of classroom teachers as associated teacher educators engaged in purposeful practice.

Such dynamic interchanges of teacher to teacher mentality extend to teacher candidates, novice classroom teachers, and teacher educators. Further, these promote the continued excitement and innovative creativity necessary and appropriate for all of our classroom educators in order to attain and exhibit consistent displays of purposeful practice in subject matter expertise, and an inherent understanding of the learning communities that integrates nuanced understandings associated with differentiated learning landscapes.

These shared understandings and expertise as well as the ability to embrace lifelong learning coupled with resources serve to fuel the excitement of transformations found in professional renewal.

The enriched key points in the three texts highlight and integrate differences within the realm of teacher education through the theoretical, data-driven, and contextual realities of teaching and learning. These underpinnings are then the basis of the transformational journey toward becoming classroom teachers that also benefit veteran teachers in the process.

This text is designated into three separate yet related books of focus:

- *Redefining Teacher Preparation: Learning From Experience in Educator Development*
- *Dynamic Principles of Professional Development: Essential Elements of Effective Teacher Preparation*
- *Teacher to Teacher Mentality: Purposeful Practice in Teacher Education*

Each text engages in intriguing frames of discussion from various regional areas of the United States of America. Further the chapters contained in each text explore the different types of school districts and parishes, including shifts from large metropolitan, independent school districts and those pertaining to smaller towns and principalities that support and engage in teacher education field-based efforts.

One of the core strengths of the teacher education profession is the integral, continuous, and highly respected field-based classroom educators who through teacher to teacher mentality formally and informally serve as associated teacher educators. Each of the texts extends and links the rich discourse beyond the bounds of the academic hallways into the teachers' classrooms, highlighting the amazing work efforts, professional dispositions of continuous engagement, nurturing efforts, and amazingly demonstrated professional kindness as displayed by classroom teachers in their roles as associated teacher educators working with university-based faculty.

The first text is titled *Redefining Teacher Preparation: Learning From Experience in Educator Development*. The chapters highlight applications and reflections of the Association of Teacher Educators' (ATE) Standards for Teacher Educators and offer conceptual frameworks and contextual realities in connections to classroom educators at all stages of their career as associated teacher educators.

The transformational nature of the teacher education process reflected in these chapters reflects a deeper understanding of the professional shifts of theory and practice dynamics within and across school district as well as university-based teacher educators. These partnerships provide vast opportunities for professional development to learn and share through contextual engagement and communication of differentiated roles and associated experiential journeys that result in enriched practice and reflection as shared throughout the authored chapters.

The text *Dynamic Principles of Professional Development: Essential Elements of Effective Teacher Preparation* focuses upon differentiated elements toward inquiry and the reflectivity of practitioners as dynamic components of professional development. The chapters explore the sense of professional development that often occurs within the context of the field-based classroom experiences and school sites, while still allowing for a metaphoric dance that represents the deep connectivity linked to more formalized professional development opportunities.

Such opportunities include the sharing of experiences and engaging of useful instructional outcomes, as well as discourse that occurs among professional educators. These elements extend beyond the conceived ivory tower and are further integrated within the learning landscape of practice that is the pre-kindergarten through 12th-grade school districts and teachers' classrooms' environmental venues.

Hence, the chapters in this text illustrate classroom teachers as associated teacher educators engaged in powerful and effective mentorships and collegial support networks within and across contexts of learning and learning how to teach. These integral processes are further intricately interconnected within multiple levels of influence and engagement that reflectively results in a continuing dialogue of understanding and impact that connects learning communities to improve practice as evidenced in the authored chapters.

The text *Teacher to Teacher Mentality: Purposeful Practice in Teacher Education* focuses upon professional discourse that revolves around induction efforts in purposeful practice and highlights dispositional understandings associated with effective teacher leaders. These elements as well as teacher to teacher mentality of teacher candidate collegial support by classroom teachers are also explored in the chapters.

These key concepts integrate and form the basis of effective collaborations between teacher candidates, classroom teachers, field-based university supervisors, and teacher education faculty that resonate in the chapters. An intriguing shift within this text are the dispositional underpinnings as framed through communities of learning, communities of practice (Wenger, 1998, 2009) as well as Wenger's more recent learning in landscapes of practice (Wenger-Trayner, Fenton-O'Creevy, Hutchinson, Kubiak, & Wenger-Trayner, 2015).

This text is offered to serve as a guiding framework that is adjustable as a useful tool toward developing and transforming pathways in meeting the professional development needs of the individual classroom teacher as associated teacher educators. It is important to emphasize that this framework has moveable components and therefore shifts to suit various contexts and levels of teacher development, including those paradigms of teacher educators at the university and beyond.

The following chapters further reflect teacher to teacher mentality as the development of an approach toward professional understanding and professionalism of teacher educators' purposeful practice within and across all levels and contexts of teacher education discourse and engagement.

REFERENCES

Wenger, E. (1998). *Communities of practice: Learning, meaning, and identity*. Cambridge, MA: Harvard University Press.

Wenger, E. (2009). A social theory of learning. In K. Illeris (Ed.), *Contemporary theories of learning: Learning theorists . . . in their own words*. New York, NY: Routledge.

Wenger-Trayner, E., Fenton-O'Creevy, M., Hutchinson, S., Kubiak, C., & Wenger-Trayner, B. (2015). *Learning in landscapes of practice: Boundaries, identify, and knowledgeability in practice-based learning*. New York, NY: Routledge.

Overview and Framework
Caroline M. Crawford and Sandra L. Hardy

Teacher to teacher mentality in teacher education at all levels encounters learning communities wherein purposeful practice may be perceived and experienced through contextual elements that shape the focus upon practical applications of skills, knowledge, and dispositions. Implications toward measures of quality as evidenced effectiveness of teacher educators including classroom teachers as associated teacher educators are integrated, sometimes seamlessly, into interrelated community paradigms as a developing conceptual framework of communities of learning (Kearney & Zuber-Skerritt, 2012; Park & So, 2014; Tam, 2015).

These dynamic shifts in paradigms of communities in practice extend to learning communities of practice (Wenger, 1998, 2009). The understanding of communities of practice is also well integrated into a landscape of practice (Wenger-Trayner et al., 2015).

The induction and continued professional support inside and outside of professional organizational contexts is vitally important toward professional engagements beyond the limitations of the school site. In recognition of the inherent needs of educators, especially novices, to work within and across experiential, supportive, and real-world school sites, inductions into learning communities of purposeful practice foster teacher to teacher mentality in professional development throughout all stages of further learning to teach.

This text focuses upon *Teacher to Teacher Mentality: Purposeful Practice in Teacher Education* with professional discourse that revolves around comprehensive induction efforts and highlights dispositional understandings associated with effective teacher leaders. Within this text, the authors explore the concepts of learning communities that promote collaborative approaches of multiple learning communities associated with professional development. This includes core elements of teacher candidates' collegial support by classroom teachers. Further, these learning communities of purposeful practice are considered in terms of real-world contexts of classroom teachers as associated teacher educators supporting the teacher to teacher mentality in professional development of educators at all levels of experience.

An intriguing shift within this text are the dispositional underpinnings as framed through communities of learning, communities of practice (Wenger, 1998, 2009), as well as Wenger's more recent learning in landscapes of practice (Wenger-Trayner et al., 2015). These key concepts integrate and form the basis of effective collaborations that resonate in the following chapters to further reflect the development of an approach toward professional understanding and professionalism of teacher educators within and across all levels and contexts of communities through learning and practice.

In chapter 1, "Learning Communities in Practice and Induction: Implications for Professional Development Organizations," Hardy brings forward the strength of approach revolving around field-based experiences to lead teacher candidates and all novices in the education arena as well as veteran educators and higher education teacher educators and administrators toward a trajectory that merges and engages in professional successes.

Hardy's work highlights an induction period that not only encompasses the multidimensional components of the teacher education practices but also supports professional development engagement and organizational support. Fostering the emerging and enhanced communities of teachers as learners is also recognized as learning communities' applaud and embrace learning and teaching of professional practice. The far-reaching implications achieved within Hardy's work are recognized as intrinsic toward the success of learning organizations, with an innovatively creative approach toward the advancement of professional development organizations in the process.

In chapter 2, "Qualities of Effective Teacher Leaders," Musselman, Patterson, and Gierhart introduce into the discussion the qualities of effective teacher leaders. The concept of teacher leaders is embraced as classroom teachers who take upon themselves the additional professional roles and responsibilities that fall within the realm of professional leadership outside the classroom environment.

These leadership roles support teacher candidates and novice classroom teachers toward enhanced levels of proficiency in the field of professional education. This discussion frames the qualities as inclusive of professional vision, co-teaching strategy implementation, and engagement, supporting professional development from differentiated perspectives and roles, professional dialogue and collegial engagement, partnerships with families while also participating in professional communities, and different presentations of professionalism. Also imperative within this frame of understanding are strategies toward growing teacher leaders by constructing a culture of leadership capacity.

In chapter 3, "As the Moments Unfold: Developing Dispositions in Student Teacher-Mentor Teacher Relationships," Davis and Fantozzi bring to the forefront the importance of mentor classroom teachers and the significant impact that is achieved upon a teacher candidate's student teaching experience. This discussion revolves around dispositions and unfolding understandings related to student candidate and mentor teacher relationships.

The work engages in a view of the mentor classroom teacher, not only from a dispositional understanding but also from a theoretical understanding of the mentorship experience and student teaching journey. Together with the perspectives and understandings of the teacher candidates, the authors bring forward a more complete picture of the complex nature of interactions and experiential support structures that develop into five phases of interaction and dispositional development.

Bromer's work in chapter 4, "An Enhanced Role for Cooperating Teachers During Student Teaching: Effective Collaboration Within a Professional Learning Community," embraces the effective collaboration impact within a professional learning community, focusing upon the enhanced role of classroom teachers as associated teacher educators throughout the student teaching experience.

Bromer highlights the effectiveness of the triangulated collaboration between the teacher candidate, the classroom educator who embraces the role of associated teacher educator, and the university supervisor; the effectiveness of the relationship is unique and positive, with a shared commitment toward reflective practice and support. Also highlighted is a need for further research as based within the interpersonal factors that support collaborative environments within the teacher preparation program, specifically toward the recognition of the vital role of classroom teachers as associated teacher educators.

Crawford and Hardy complete this text with their emphasis in chapter 5, "Critical Understandings of Classroom Teachers as Associated Teacher Educators on Learning Landscapes of Practice: A Case Study Approach," upon a critical understanding of classroom teachers as associated teacher educators, with specific focus upon a case study approach toward a better understanding of learning to teach within a school-based practice.

This case study approach offered a qualitative evaluation of classroom teachers at the elementary school and high school levels of professional teaching engagement. The work engages the real-world multiple viewpoints of 32 classroom teachers, framed within an effort toward more fully understanding classroom teacher's discourse and reflections when requested to respond to specific open-ended questions centered upon suggestions and perceptions associated with teacher candidates, university faculty, novice classroom teachers, and the profession of teaching.

The thematic approach to the research questions and associated verbatim quotes of the classroom teachers engage in the development of a stronger understanding of the field-based teacher education process and further define classroom teachers as associated teacher educators.

REFERENCES

Kearney, J., & Zuber-Skerritt, O. (2012). From learning organization to learning community: Sustainability through lifelong learning. *The Learning Organization, 19*(5), 400–413.

Park, M., & So, K. (2014). Opportunities and challenges for teacher professional development: A case of collaborative learning community in South Korea. *International Education Studies, 7*(7), 96. Retrieved from http://www.ccsenet.org/journal/index.php/ies/article/viewFile/36243/21310

Tam, A.C.F. (2015). The role of a professional learning community in teacher change: A perspective from beliefs and practices. *Teachers and Teaching, 21*(1), 22–43.

Wenger, E. (1998). *Communities of practice: Learning, meaning, and identity*. Cambridge, MA: Harvard University Press.

Wenger, E. (2009). A social theory of learning. In K. Illeris (Ed.), *Contemporary theories of learning: Learning theorists . . . in their own words*. New York, NY: Routledge.

Wenger-Trayner, E., Fenton-O'Creevy, M., Hutchinson, S., Kubiak, C., & Wenger-Trayner, B. (2015). *Learning in landscapes of practice: Boundaries, identify, and knowledgeability in practice-based learning*. New York, NY: Routledge.

Chapter One

Learning Communities in Practice and Induction

Implications for Professional Development Organizations

Sandra L. Hardy

ABSTRACT

The focus of this chapter is on the advancing role of professional development organizations as possessing the capacity to support and enhance the introduction to the field trajectory for educators and administrators in schools and institutions of higher learning from novice to veteran. Induction is defined as encompassing the continuum from teacher preparation through professional development (Feiman-Nemser, 2010). The multidimensional components of teacher preparation and induction culminate with implications for professional development that serves novices while fostering a community of teachers as learners (Feiman-Nemser, 2010).

KEYWORDS

Associated teacher educators, collaboration, contexts, individual, induction, learning communities in practice, mentor, novice, pedagogical content knowledge, pre existing beliefs, professional development, professional development organizations, retention

PROFESSIONAL DEVELOPMENT ORGANIZATIONS AND LEARNING COMMUNITIES IN PRACTICE: AN OVERVIEW

Professional development organizations are identified as a vital component in the frameworks of effectively constructed preparation linked to induction in the development of the individual teacher as learner. As such, professional development organizations are defined as those organizations that provide far-reaching and meaningful opportunities for individual growth on a personal and professional level. This development applies to teachers, administrators, and others of all learning communities.

Therefore, professional development organizations serve the novice teacher and administrator preparation programs, as well as higher education educators and administrators and those who support them as members of learning communities in practice in the contexts where they learn and teach. Further, induction improvements in this regard seek to simultaneously incorporate the required elements to the climate and resources of a particular learning to teach context (Feiman-Nemser, 2010; Flores, 2010; Smith & Finch, 2010) and consequently shape learning communities in practice.

Professional learning communities both define and are defined by the social infrastructures connected to a learning institution coupled with the ontogeny of involved individuals and mutual appreciation with respect to diversity (Wiseman, Arroyo, & Richter, 2013). Communities of practice recognize learning as individualistically evolving to address the whole person through multiple interactions with processes that clarifies the learner and resolves to strengthen the associated connections (Lave & Wenger, 2015).

Therefore, communities of practice have the capacity to transcend organizational boundaries to enrich and enhance learning (Wenger, 2008). Professional learning communities and communities in practice in their unity largely describe learning communities in practice.

Professional development organizations thus function within and across varied contexts of multiple learning communities in practice. The socially situated constructivist perspective of teacher as a learner recognizes that multiple contexts of learning contribute to the individual teachers' constructs in and from collaboration with others (Borko, 2004; Palinscar, 1998; Putnam & Borko, 2000). Hence, synergistic assistance is an essential attribute of school culture that strengthens all induction components (Flores, 2010).

In addition to contexts, teacher retention is enhanced through the joint efforts of schools and universities to foster novices' acquisition of pedagogical content knowledge defined as how learners learn and contexts in which learning occurs (Shulman, 1986). In the process of further professional development, teachers often encounter their preexisting beliefs about learning and teaching.

Also in the course of induction with other teachers, mentors, university teacher educators, and administrators are all essential as associated teacher educators of the learning communities in practice. Each of these roles is explored in the text, relative to teacher induction and retention. The induction needs of administrators and higher education faculty are also presented.

Throughout the chapter the potential services of professional development organizations are emphasized. Further, areas in need of research concerning learning communities in practice, induction, as well as professional development organizations are presented.

Learning Communities in Practice: Induction and Professional Development Organizations

Given the tremendous challenges of education today with the continued high attrition of teachers in a complex education culture of increasing diversity, the need for fostering collaboration while developing the individual teacher and learner within and across local and global contexts is critical. Of all the professions, the education profession holds enormous personal and professional intricacies for the novice (Iordandides & Vyroni, 2013).

Effective induction of novice teachers as well as new administrators in all educational settings including higher education is essential as is the connectivity of collaboration therein. The induction processes in order to have substantial impact require intensely extensive internal and external networks. The structural foundation upholds the individual teacher as a learner, the individual as a member of a community, and the relation of one community to another in learning and in practice. Thus, functionality of induction in this regard for both short-term and long-term results is defined in part by learning in association with and from others as professional learning communities.

Learning Communities in Practice Defined

Communities of practice recognize learning as individualistically evolving to address the whole person through multiple interactions with structures that clarifies the learner and resolves to strengthen the associated connections (Lave & Wenger, 2015). Therefore, communities of practice have the potential to transcend organizational boundaries to enrich and enhance learning (Wenger, 2008).

Professional learning communities and communities of practice are unified in further learning and learning to teach across all levels and forms of educational processes professionally intertwined and thereby describe learning communities in practice. Learning communities require resources and serve as a resource with the learning that occurs in classrooms serving as an example.

Therein learning communities engage in practice and are largely self-directed in that respect (Wenger, 2008). Broad-based and well-supported multiple learning communities in practice of induction efforts encompass and interlink the ingenuities, talents, inventiveness, and capabilities of classrooms, schools, higher learning institutions, and continued professional development opportunities. Each learning community exists in relational contexts of multiple other constructed communities.

Learning Communities in Practice: Induction

The basic framework of induction for learning communities in practice consists of honoring the autonomy of teachers, individually and collectively, as learners in all stages of professional development and educational circumstances. Learning communities in practice may be coordinated and sustained long before and after each induction experience. Individual educators are interconnected with other classroom teachers as associated teacher educators through complex support systems.

The emphasis is on working together to develop the individual and then also the individual in connection to others, including colleagues, which encourages the professional educator to flourish and be in continuous renewal. (See Figure 1.1.) Thus, induction includes the additional acquisition of knowledge, skills, and attitudes which are more fully attained through participating in thriving learning communities in practice. To orchestrate and implement individualized induction of this magnitude requires organization of time in careful measure with other valuable components. These needed elements are often greatly lacking in the substance and sustenance of current induction and professional development efforts concerning the individual teacher as learner.

Figure 1.1 illustrates the individual throughout the learning to teach continuum. The black outlined arrows represent learning communities in practice.

Induction experiences have the potential to frame the future of the education profession as it will be practiced for the next 30 years (Moir & Gless, 2001). Piecemeal induction in isolation without connection to other induction

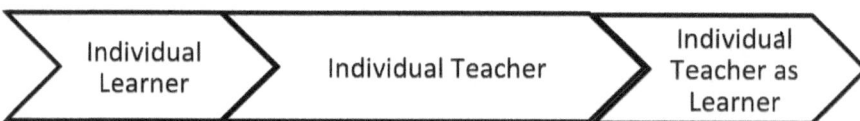

Figure 1.1. Teacher as Individual.

programs, educators, administrators, and resources is incomplete. Communities of learning in practice stand to benefit from a much broader standing, farther-reaching, well-coordinated perspective of information and available assistance derived from local, state, national, and international sources. Such a framework and knowledge base would enhance induction experiences of professional educators as individual learners in the contexts of learning communities in practice.

Definition and Implications for Professional Development Organizations

"Induction must be seen as an organizational and professional responsibility shared by many, including new and experienced academics, faculties, departments, institutions and professional associations" (Martinez, 2008, p. 35). Professional development organizations connect preservice, novice, veteran teachers, mentors, administrators, and higher education faculty and administrators from across the nation and around the world to learn from and support one another.

Professional development organizations bring forth standards to guide professional program development through collaboration, and scholarship of teaching and vision of the teacher education profession (Standards for Associated Teacher Educators: http://www.ate1.org/pubs/uploads/tchredstds0308.pdf).

While there are many professional development organizations, the focus in this chapter is upon the tremendous largely untapped potential of those which serve preservice through higher education communities of learning in practice to support induction and thereby also significantly impact comprehensive professional development.

Professional development organizations have an excellent vantage point to know the contexts of many induction programs throughout districts, states, and regions as well as national and even international efforts. As such they are in a key position to serve through interlinking schools, educators, teacher educators, and administrators across grade levels and other contexts and circumstances.

The services they offer may facilitate the support of learning from other members of an expanding learning community in the practice of effective induction. Further, in the process professional development organizations have the potential to serve, strengthen, and develop each novice, which in turn enriches individual effectiveness and as a result further defines these learning communities in practice and induction.

The professional literature is sparse and lacks attention to professional development organizations in their support of learning communities in practice and induction. Therefore, this chapter identifies the essential components of induction of classroom teachers, mentors, university teacher educators, and administrators as associated teacher educators from an immediate local and a far-reaching global perspective.

The significance of connections to multiple learning communities in practice through professional development organizations is explored. With the vast inevitability of conflicting expectations and unrealistic limitations in various aspects of planning and implementation, professional development organizations, in the fullness of their role, bridge differences and unite common purposes through shared means to develop both the individual and consequently the community of learning in practice. Throughout this chapter the focus of induction into learning communities in practice is upheld by the valued foundational girding of professional development organizations.

Key Concepts of the Chapter

This chapter presents through the lens of learning communities in practice each segment which follows. Although the primary focus is induction of the novice teacher, the chapter also addresses the induction of mentors, administrators, and higher education teacher educators. Additionally, each section concludes with the corresponding implications for professional development organizations.

First, induction is examined through learning communities in practice. Second, the contexts of induction and learning communities in practice are explored. Next, the impact of beliefs and the acquisition of pedagogical content knowledge in further learning to teach are considered. This is then followed by mentoring in learning communities in practice. Finally, the implications of induction in global and local contexts connected to communities of learning in practice as supported by professional development organizations are presented and areas for further exploration and research are highlighted.

LEARNING COMMUNITIES IN PRACTICE: TEACHER INDUCTION AND PROFESSIONAL DEVELOPMENT ORGANIZATIONS

Teacher induction encompasses the continuum of learning to teach from early teacher preparation through professional development (Feiman-Nemser, 2010). Local induction shapes global induction and back again in an upward and outward spiral of learning communities in practice that may be greatly enhanced and sustained through the services of professional development organizations. Each induction experience carries the potential to shape the individual novice personally and professionally and thereby contributes in general and specific terms to the working definition of learning communities in practice.

Novice teachers often graduate from a university teacher education program and enter into their first few years of teaching full of fresh ideas, high hopes, and aspiring dreams. Many novice teachers quickly discover they are in need of full induction supports ideally featuring collaboration from several levels of education professionals. Associated teacher educators include other novice teachers, veteran classroom teachers, university teacher educators, administrators, and other professional education specialists.

However, some of the educators and administrators the novice turns to call upon may themselves be lacking in a multitude of induction knowledge and other elements stemming from their own early professional learning experiences. The potential void of professionally guided entry into the profession perhaps generated an isolated feeling of abandonment in the novice. Crippled by the circumstances, these ill-supported novices limp along gathering bits and pieces of professional development here and there along the way as best they are able.

In further learning to teach, most novice teachers seek collaborative backing from their fellow novice teachers, more experienced teachers, higher education teacher educators, other educational professionals, and administrators as associated teacher educators for support when possible. Though not frequently available for a variety of reasons, novice teachers often express the need for university teacher educators to participate in induction processes with direct involvement in the field (Hardy, 2012).

The section that follows examines the need for guided entry into the education profession of university teacher educators concerning their own unique learning communities in practice. Further without induction into their earlier teaching careers or into their current field in higher education, teacher educators may not be well prepared to support the induction of novice teachers in the field.

LEARNING COMMUNITIES IN PRACTICE: UNIVERSITY TEACHER EDUCATORS AND INDUCTION

Novice practitioners at all levels benefit from university faculty support to implement what they learned at the university. Otherwise, new staff may be engulfed in the demands of the system in place (Sullivan & Glanz, 2000). Novice teachers may discover that their unique journey from a university preservice teacher education student to new teacher in a school generates feelings of inadequacy, isolation, and even some sense of abandonment as they long for continued contact and involvement in the field from university teacher educators.

The communication may be as simple and remote as e-mail or as direct and involved as visiting them in their new school and classroom to observe and be observed modeling instructional strategies, offering feedback, and other areas of professional development.

Higher education teacher preparation instructors have the potential to serve as a source of support for novice teachers from teacher preparation through induction in context (Chubbick, Clift, Allard, & Quinlan, 2001; Feiman-Nemser, 2001; Kagan, 1992; Massey, 2006; Sullivan & Glanz, 2000; Wisniewski, 2004). Novice teachers perceive the need for university teacher educators to be an integral component in all stages along the way.

"University teacher educators' role from pre-service through induction would entail their presence to a greater extent in the field" (Hardy, 2012, p. 277). Hence, teacher educators' role in the field requires their working with schools' induction programs to jointly deliver seamless support to novice and mentor teachers (Bergeron, 2008). University teacher educators in the classroom may offer such supports as modeling writing instruction, being observed and observing, feedback and reflection, inviting collaboration, and navigating context.

Higher Education Induction

While novice teachers may express a need for university teacher educators to be more involved and present in their first few years of teaching, newer university teacher educators frequently fend for themselves without an adequate induction experience into the learning communities in practice of higher education. Most novice higher education teacher educators learn through practice with a sort of casual apprentice-type approach when fortunate enough to have any induction experience (Murray, 2005).

As Knowles and Cole so aptly explain, "Though the contexts and roles associated with working in postsecondary institutions are vastly different from those in the elementary and secondary schools and classrooms of the beginning teachers we study, the similarities to our experiences as neophytes are striking" (Knowles & Cole, 2015, p. 27).

It is important to recognize the need for induction of faculty into higher education contexts (Knowels & Cole, 2015). Learning communities in practice at all levels are influenced by the action and reaction of individuals within that immediate circle as well as those from other learning communities. Each university teacher educator who extends support to a novice teacher in the field creates the greater possibility of other teachers learning from that classroom teacher as an associated teacher educator.

What one university teacher educator learns in turn teaches many others. Further, such support increases the likelihood of acquiring further pedagogical knowledge which then also contributes to student achievement as well as increases the retention of effective teachers in the field. These and other previously mentioned aspects of induction support will be expounded upon in subsequent sections of this chapter.

Therefore, higher education teacher educators themselves require adequate support so as to provide induction backing for the novices they encounter. Induction is advised for teacher educators and new higher education instructors in all fields (Martinez, 2008). Studies indicate that novices, experienced teachers, and university teacher educators share in common the appreciation of learning in the clinical setting with structured support more than any other teacher preparation component (Feiman-Nemser, 2001; Goodlad, 2004). With that awareness comes also an enhanced definition of professionalism that continues to set the tone for practice of university teacher educators in the field of induction.

Implications for Professional Development Organizations

Professional development organizations from advantageous vantage points can tailor support to the circumstances of programs and teachers involved at all levels and contexts. This also emphasizes the importance of professional development organizations creating opportunities for novices to participate in well-established communities of learning in practice that involves the collaboration of teachers in all levels of experience, from various contexts in other schools and classrooms, as well as from the insight and guidance of administrators, mentors, and higher education teacher educators.

Without the influence, framework, and coordination from professional development organizations, however, the continued learning to teach experiences of induction is all too often found to be without the supportive participation of higher education faculty to enhance instruction with adequate acquisition of additional pedagogical content knowledge.

Higher education contexts with internal and external pressures greatly define communities of practice and to what extent those practices extend to K-12 schools as well as the form these services take when they are available (James, 2007). Consequently, higher education's communities of learning in practice then contribute to the learning of their communities which cross over into learning communities in practice of K-12 teachers, administrators, and other education professionals and back, and again.

While these two learning communities, K-12 and higher education, have much in common, there may also be conflicting circumstances. For example, in certain content areas such as writing instruction, some novice teachers are hopeful that such available interaction may compensate for what they perceive as a lack of prior preparation in their teacher education programs as well as build upon what they have learned (Hardy, 2012).

University-based teacher educators are also an essential part of learning communities in practice that fosters collaborative support for novice teachers and benefits professional development of other teachers as well. Each novice teacher and university teacher educator (who may also be a novice) brings to the process the individual teacher as learner and their corresponding beliefs, attitudes, and expectations.

Furthermore, the interaction of the two individuals also greatly contributes to the dynamics and establishes boundaries while achieving goals. Obviously limitations of time and other resources make the full participation of university teacher educators in even the best of circumstances limited in the scope of the field.

Professional development organizations may draw on their membership to have the insight of knowledge concerning the content and practices of multiple teacher education and induction programs in their respective contexts.

Furthermore, they are poised to unite and call upon resources to locally and globally inform, develop, and sustain learning communities in practice concerning university-based teacher educators in the field. Such a far-reaching perspective may increase the segments of time and other valuable elements for postsecondary teacher educators to be more visibly involved in actively engaging novices, including administrative novices and others in the induction field.

Research is needed in higher education induction pertaining to teacher educators in several areas as follows:

- To determine the perceptions from novice teachers, administrators, and university faculty and administration as to the functional role of teacher educators from university teacher preparation through induction contexts.
- Further, research in this area may help to clarify to what extent the induction of faculty into higher education teacher preparation programs addresses their induction needs.
- Additionally, research is needed to better understand teacher educators' service in the field of induction generally, and their service in working with school districts and administration on behalf of novice teachers specifically.
- Research also may further define the effects of learning communities in practice in both higher education and elementary and secondary schools pertaining to teacher educators and induction.
- Research is needed to examine the short-term and long-term effects of professional development organizations in working in support of higher education teacher education programs as well as their contribution to teacher educators' efforts in the induction process.

Learning Communities in Practice: Administration and Induction

Administrators serve in multiple areas as leaders in induction. In addition to novice teacher support and teacher leader, they contribute to the culture of the school or context, and advance the efforts of mentors (Wood, 2005). The ongoing decision-making process of the administration in addressing the many aspects and issues throughout the induction process contributes to the processes which establish effective practices for the education community.

Therefore, the administration speaks through its actions and choices as to the value of induction for the novice teacher and for all novices, school nurses, counselors, social workers, and novice administrators in their school.

Like teachers, administrators also benefit from an immediate and extended collaboration of other school administrators, novice and veteran administrators, and higher education administration faculty to share ideas, learn resources, and gain support as a learning community in practice.

Induction of administrators, teachers, and teacher educators each reinforces the other. The arrows represent professional development organizations serving to link and support.

Administrative involvement and commitment is paramount to motivate and advance learning communities in practice. Administrators' direction and coordination may include the participation of many teachers and others

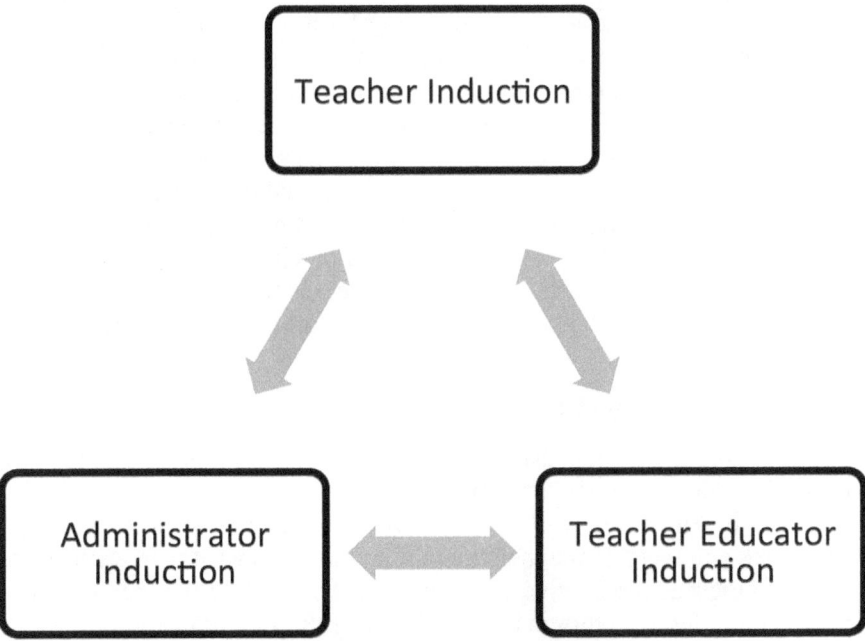

Figure 1.2. Induction of Learning Communities in Practice

in the planning, implementation, evaluation, and development of induction. The collaboration needed in all forms of novice induction, special education teachers included, requires administrative support (Prather-Jones, 2011; Youngs, Jones, & Low, 2011).

Administrators hold the keys to unlock doors, arrange and rearrange schedules, locate and relocate classrooms, and provide other means to foster collaboration of veteran and novice teachers, university faculty, and administration to enrich induction. Furthermore, administrators may bring to this dynamic process an awareness of the unique needs of each teacher so as to personalize induction to the individual's professional development. With this awareness, the administrator is more likely to find ways to make resources of time, space, and materials available to best meet the needs of teachers in order to enhance student and teacher learning and retention.

With administration establishing the climate to support induction, each component becomes a vital link connected throughout learning communities in practice. These dynamic interchanges of practice and discourse construct and reconstruct into vast internal and external networks of professionals. When one member of learning communities in practice is given professional development opportunities, all benefit, and conversely the reverse is also true.

Bringing university-based teacher educators into schools to work side by side with classroom teachers as associated teacher educators is a tall order. School administration may have certain ideas and beliefs pertaining to induction in this regard. These perceptions may be partly influenced from their perspectives and responsibilities in their assigned roles as school administrators which afford them a more in-depth understanding potentially of the subtle nuances and budgetary constraints in the immediate and, to an extent, the future contexts of their school as a learning community.

University teacher educators and university administrators may have suggestions and expectations that deviate from those of the school administration. Therefore, effective communication of vision as to purpose, roles, expectations, limitations, and goals with respect to the induction process from both the university administration and school administration is essential.

Administration Induction

Administrators are often overwhelmed and isolated from their peers as well. For novice administrators the experience is frequently intensified. Novice administrators are receptive to professional development such as coaching, role model, and mentors that help them operationalize what they learned and put it into their administrative practice (Bodger, 2011). While inexperienced and veteran administrators may attend a workshop or professional conference on occasion, these professional development experiences may be often located remotely and offer fragmented knowledge that lacks insight and connectivity to the multiple contexts of the realities encountered in practice.

Entrenched contextual underpinnings of current circumstances, identified individualized professional development needs, and mobilization of available resources interdependently drive administrative improvements of induction efforts of learning communities in practice. School administrators benefit from an internship experience coupled with support across contexts while linking university learning with school application (Bodger, 2011).

Novice administrators also benefit from induction into the school and learning communities in practice. New administrators may be faced with the challenges of providing induction support services to several novice teachers in addition to their other responsibilities. Therefore, it must be emphasized that induction of all education professionals is essential.

Certainly, administrative induction though critical is often overlooked or minimal in the first few years on the job. Yet, administrators are expected to play a strong role in the induction process of all novices in their building and district.

Implications for Professional Development Organizations

Professional development organizations have the potential to offer educational expertise from a wide range of learning to teach areas of induction that tailors to the uniqueness of teachers, administrators, schools, and universities in allocating resources to best address the learning to teach needs in contexts where they teach. Likewise, induction of administrators is also in need of the support services of professional development organizations.

Further research is needed in the area of administration induction and the role of administration in induction as well.

- In what ways do learning communities in practice contribute to the induction of administrators?
- What are the induction needs of administrators in preparing them to support novice teachers?
- How can professional development organizations incorporate school and university administration induction knowledge, resources, and needs to best meet the induction needs of the individual administrator in the contexts of their school?
- What do novices, veteran, mentor teachers perceive as the role of the administration in induction?
- How can professional development organizations and learning communities in practice contribute to supporting administration to best support individual teachers in unique learning to teach contexts?

LEARNING COMMUNITIES IN PRACTICE: INDUCTION AND CONTEXTS

The induction roles of other teachers, university teacher educators, and administrators as members of learning communities in practice are enhanced when supported by adjustable frameworks. The induction experience may benefit the novice more substantially with the help of professional development organizations. Emphasis pertains to jointly conceivable efforts to develop, enrich, and promote induction processes encountered by the individual novice situated in unique local and global contexts.

Global learning communities in practice are valued when recognized in professional discourse that exchanges in creative ideas pertaining to resource management and other challenges encountered to be resolved in even well-positioned, centrally located schools. Perhaps this is critical to a far greater extent in remote impoverished educational settings (Sargent, 2015).

Learning communities in practice strive through layers of comprehensive inward and outward networks to support each member in their introduction to the education profession beginning in preparation programs and extending beyond the initial entry and the first few years which follow. The school administration, the school's overall climate, and classroom teachers as peer associated teacher educators are socially derived and contribute to professional development (Johnson, 2015).

However, it is equally important to emphasize that the membership to the communities of learning in practice does not de-emphasize the personal aspect of learning in the midst of situation, circumstance, context, and norms. In fact, the individual impacts his or her own learning while shaping communities of learning in practice (Billett, 2007).

The individual teacher as learner is therefore valued and brings certain qualities and values that shape induction experiences to acquire and apply knowledge, skills, collaboration, and reflection in developing practice. Each community of learning in practice exists within and through acts of responses throughout layers of learning, knowing, and change. The socially situated constructivist perspective of teacher as learner recognizes multiple contexts of learning that contribute to the individual teacher's constructs in the process of and as a result of enriched opportunities for professional development through collaboration (Borko, 2004; Palincsar, 1998; Putnam & Borko, 2000).

Some further learning to teach contexts subscribe to a given situation, and other scenarios may be found and experienced more generally as common. Yet, even with the best of efforts in utilizing available sources, teacher induction from the novice teachers' perspective may be somehow inadequate. The induction experience for novice teachers extends from field experiences and student teaching to the first few years of teaching.

Well-developed and sustained learning communities in practice possess the potential to impact novice teacher induction as well as induction in general. These systemic structures acknowledge the context the novice is placed deliberately into and speaks to how the community in practice values him or her (Henry, Bastian, & Fortner, 2011). These principles in practice apply to novices in all levels of education, including primary, secondary, and postsecondary schools.

Obviously, better-prepared and better-supported university teacher educators, as well as school and university administrators, require well-established induction programs in their areas of expertise. Such induction experiences on all levels of education serve to provide the foundational tools to situationally navigate and more fully implement knowledge and skills induction as associated teacher educators in all contexts and circumstances.

Learning communities in their practice improve upon comprehensive induction programs through the active participation of novice teachers, administrators, teacher educators, and other teachers (Luft, Neakrase, Adams, & Bang, 2010).

Conceptually the implications are that each individual carries out his or her responsibilities throughout learning to teach experiences in his or her respectful domain as required to become a functional member of learning communities in practice. The contextual induction components include important variables pertaining to each situation of further learning to teach through practice. Some of these variances may be attributable to prior learning and continued acquisition of pedagogical content knowledge, frequency, degree, and type of individual guidance coupled with authenticity of support with an access to available, preferred, and continuous professional development. Contextual induction components such as colleagues, technology, and professional development organizations each make contributions as well.

Contexts of colleagues. Elements of teacher preparation that the novice perceives as lacking such as in the area of writing instruction are then learned while also continuing to learn to teach during the induction period. In the immediate learning to teach context of the novice teacher's first few years of teaching, novices often turn the great resource they find in other teachers.

The proximity of other teachers as associated teacher educators provides the potential for frequent interaction with an element of caring and sharing of resources and ideas. Those teachers are likely to be most accessible, but the critical importance of other classroom teachers in other contexts as associated teacher educators is also worthy of recognition of their potential contributions. The central core of teachers within the immediate learning to teach setting are also surrounded by other teachers in similar as well as vastly different circumstances united as a learning community in practice.

Technology in contexts. Contexts for learning to teach are many and ideally extend well beyond the classroom and school to incorporate teachers from other schools, administrators, mentors, and former university teacher educators for induction support in general and of the individual specifically. The impacts of contexts may expand to include the hardships of poverty and other social and economical variables. Such variables contribute to unequal opportunities in teaching and learning (Schmidt, Burroughs, Zoido, & Houang, 2015).

Internet global connections make possible learning communities in practice with the capacity to extensively enrich and transcend most geographic and economical parameters. Immediate and expanded, face-to-face, and cyber interactions are best respectfully mindful to cultural similarities and differences in learning and teaching.

Professional Development Organizations and Contexts

The multidimensional elements of an individual's induction experience and situation frequently converge and connect. Learning communities in practice span the professional education continuum of teachers as learners. The complexity of contexts in induction programs benefits from the broad-based integrative services of professional development organizations. These include but are not limited to operating within the realities of multiple layers of contexts, locating and applying available resources efficiently and effectively, and fostering enhanced collaboration.

Professional development organizations view communities of learning in practice with a wide lens to encompass schools and universities, faculty and administration as associated teacher educators in the contexts of induction. Professional development organizations link one context to another while not losing sight of the influence of individual novice teacher's preexisting beliefs as teacher and learner in the induction process.

Areas of further research pertaining to contexts and induction are vast. Here are just a few.

- How does the context of technology most impact further learning to teach?
- What are the perspectives of novice, veteran, and mentor teachers concerning how professional development organizations might best address their professional development needs in the contexts where they teach?
- What do teachers and administrators perceive as the most effective ways to broaden their learning communities in practice through professional development organizations pertaining to contexts and colleagues?

Learning to Teach: Beliefs and the Acquisition of Pedagogical Content Knowledge

Within the complexity of induction are also the factors of veteran teacher, mentor teacher, administrator, university teacher educator, and novice teachers' beliefs, prior experiences, and expectations of themselves and one another in the induction process. Experienced well-seasoned teachers may approach a learning to teach situation differently in comparison to the novice who brings fresh ideas from the university with limited exposure to applying these concepts in the field.

For example, the application of new technology to the classroom may be on the horizon for the novice who just learned this last spring. But, for the teacher of 20 years, the change may not be so easily assimilated or accommodated.

The other teachers in the immediate and expanded learning community also bring a component of their beliefs, experience, and expectations to the process that may help or hinder induction and subsequent professional development for all concerned. Among the many needs of novice teachers is the continued acquisition of pedagogical content knowledge. Pedagogical content knowledge incorporates knowledge of how learners learn and of the contexts in which learning is to occur (Shulman, 1986).

What teachers derive from their teacher preparation experiences and education contributes to their effectiveness in their first few years of teaching (Bishop, Brownell, Klingner, Leko, & Galman, 2010). Learning to teach from teacher preparation through induction and continued professional development highlights the novice in search of additional pedagogical content knowledge.

The quest to learn how to teach certain subject matter, such as the instruction of writing, during the induction period will often be attributed by novices to areas not sufficiently addressed in formal teacher education programs (Hardy, 2012). However, even with extensive preservice preparation in content-specific domains, many novices still continue to seek additional knowledge and skills long after formal teacher preparation as they consistently strive to improve their practice.

Learning communities and further learning to teach. Novice teachers obtain content-specific pedagogy as well as pedagogy in general through a combination of an individual's formal course work, associated experience in the field, and continued professional development shared with other teachers. Of course, the significance of the contexts pertaining to teaching and the relationships of those contexts to pedagogical knowledge acquisition are substantial (Pardo, 2006).

Collectively, the overall beliefs of most teachers in a school pertaining to learning and teaching permeate the learning community therein and subsequently may contribute to altering beliefs of individuals over time. The professional literature not only points to the importance of the acquisition of pedagogical content knowledge in professional learning communities but also refers to the significance of challenging existing assumptions pertaining to such knowledge for teaching and student learning (Bausmith & Barry, 2011). Novice teachers are in a precarious position to both question the status quo and acclimate to the existing educational climate.

Encountering Existing Beliefs and Prior Learning Experiences

After graduation, novice teachers experience other contexts of learning in their first few years of teaching in which they once again encounter their own beliefs about learning and teaching. Learning to teach in context as practicing novice teachers, teacher educators, or administrators may be in opposition with the preferred methods and avenues of the prodigy in accessing professional development.

What is gathered from further learning to teach opportunities varies and is partially dependent upon the interpretation of the novice as well as based on general perceptions by the vast differences of learning communities in practice within and across circumstances. As novice teachers enter the first few years of teaching, they encounter many contextual elements such as school culture, resources, and expectations which may challenge the novice's perspectives. Research suggests teachers benefit from acknowledging their current beliefs (Wideen, Mayer-Smith, & Moon 1998).

The many experiences in learning to teach bring reflections of how one was taught in schools and universities when participating in those communities of learners in practice. As a teacher believes learning occurs so shall they teach (Cuban, 1993). One of the first contexts of learning is in what novice teachers experienced as students in early childhood, elementary, middle, and secondary schools.

These recollections shape beliefs as a result of many impressions that are formed about learning and teaching. Some beliefs may be firmly entrenched and relate to certain content areas (Zeichner, Tabachnick, & Densmore, 1987). Thus, preexisting beliefs about learning and instruction are often reflected in the teaching practice of novice educators and stem from how they as students were taught. Novice teachers find themselves teaching as they were taught by carefully selecting to emulate the better instruction they both observed and participated in as students (Hardy, 2012).

Thus, in seeking to attain further pedagogical content knowledge, teachers may need to construct and reconstruct instruction that deviates from these prior learning experiences (Hammerness et al., 2005). Similarly, existing beliefs about collaboration and mentoring may also influence a teacher's professional development.

These assorted aspects of beliefs about learning may hinder the novice teacher's efforts to acquire additional pedagogical content knowledge in areas they feel are most needed such as the instruction of writing (Troia & Maddox, 2004). Evidence of inadequate preservice programs in this regard illuminates an even more critical aspect that well supported continued learning to teach professional development opportunities in content areas such as writing be made available to practicing teachers (Gilbert & Graham, 2010). Well-prepared teachers of writing are the responsibility of teacher education programs and school districts (Kiuhara, Hawken, & Graham, 2009). This carries over to other content areas as well.

Implications for Professional Development Organizations

To more adequately meet the needs of each novice teacher as learner requires the orchestration of comprehensively individualized induction experiences and supports that acknowledge their existing beliefs. Induction of this caliber of excellence requires the well-coordinated cooperation of multiple learning communities in practice as schools and universities and beyond.

Within these learning communities the teacher educators and administrators individually contribute and jointly move to utilize resources that best provide the site-based university connected level of professional development for each novice. Clearly, the frameworks for effective induction of this magnitude require a vast array of assistance to locate, connect, and assimilate available knowledge and resources. Such far-reaching induction building and delivery of services with full backing of implementation and assessment are perhaps possible to realize through utilizing the assistance of professional development organizations.

All professional work is complex and demanding (Hargreaves & Fullan, 2000).Common ground links similarities while reaching across differences to build bridges from university teacher preparation programs to school district induction through high standards of professional development. Bringing together school and university to attain greater pedagogical content knowledge and acknowledge teaching and learning beliefs in the process is just one of the dynamic infrastructures that may to be brought to fruition through the services of professional development organizations.

The process and outcomes of professional development organizations coordinate an induction interface of higher education teacher educators, administrators, and classroom teachers as associated teacher educators. The interlinking of multiple learning communities in practice expands and enriches each circle of professional educators, which advances the knowledge and skills of the individual teacher to challenge existing conceptions and in turn strengthen and shape induction to promote collaboration and teacher retention.

Areas for further research are as follows:

- In what ways can professional development organizations work with schools and universities to individualize induction so that the acquisition of pedagogical knowledge is enhanced in the process? How would this framework apply to content-specific pedagogical knowledge acquisition?
- Do learning communities in practice shape novice teachers' beliefs over time? If so, how?
- In what ways are novice teachers' beliefs influenced by mentor teachers' beliefs in a learning community in practice? How is this demonstrated?

Learning Communities in Practice: Enhancing Collaboration and Retention

Attrition and subsequent shortages of education professionals are not new. The problem of retaining new teachers has never been more critical than it is currently during this time of enormous teacher turn-over (Freiberg, 2000). The components of collaboration offered in the first year of teaching are especially critical to retain effective teachers as teacher attrition is most likely to occur before the second year of teaching (Graves, 2002; Ingersoll & Strong, 2011).

Learning communities in practice include classroom teachers, higher education teacher educators, and elementary, secondary, and post-secondary administrators who value the induction support of novices. This includes novice administrators and novice university teacher educators who are far too frequently overlooked and receive no induction of their own.

Induction of effective educators encourages novices to continue their development of pedagogical content knowledge and skills and promotes positive collegial relations among teachers and between teachers and administrators. Peer teachers, administration, and the overall climate of the school are highly valued to teachers and consequently increase the likelihood of teacher development and retention which therefore may benefit student progress in learning (Johnson, Kraft, & Papay, 2012).

Teachers who graduate from university teacher preparation programs and who partake in continued professional development have a greater likelihood of continuing to teach (Smith, 2007). Aspects of desired professional development in the induction period linked to retention beyond the first year of teaching highlight the acquisition of additional pedagogical content knowledge.

Therefore, it is most significant to further define an understanding of subject matter to include enhanced content-specific knowledge and skills of each teacher while also promoting a learning environment conducive to individual progress and effective teacher retention (Swanson, 2010).

Again, pedagogical knowledge and skills are sought in specific subject areas novices may find lacking in their teacher preparation and education such as the instruction of writing (Gilbert & Graham, 2010). The development of such knowledge and skills is strengthened through novice teachers' participation in university-school linked methods courses, engagement in opportunities for practice, and observing other teachers' implementation of such knowledge and skills in their practice (Hardy, 2012).

Furthermore, novice teachers especially benefit from and greatly appreciate direct observation of their instruction with associated immediate and constructive feedback with suggestions for improvement (Ingersoll, Merrill, & May, 2014). Observations and feedback are best delivered from many associated teacher educators including but not limited to novice, mentor, and veteran teachers, administrators, and higher education. Further emphasis on realizing and expanding the role of higher education is paramount in this regard.

University Teacher Educators: Enhance Collaboration and Retention

Given the strong connection between the acquisition of pedagogical content knowledge and skills and teacher retention through methods courses, observation, and feedback, the contribution of university teacher educators from preservice through induction is paramount. University teacher educators may contribute, among other attributes, a greater emphasis on pedagogical knowledge and skills development in their methods courses and field experiences.

Further, learning communities in practice recognize the induction need for university teacher educators to increase and extend their observations of novice teachers in preservice programs through at least the first year of teaching with feedback and guidance in the field. Such observations and suggestions for improvement are greatly enhanced through university teacher educators' modeling of the knowledge and skills novice teachers are to acquire. Further, university teacher educators are expected to be knowledgeable concerning local districts' available resources and needs of novice teachers pertaining to specific subject matter and skills (Luft et al., 2010).

Of course, the individual university teacher educators may approach such field-based course connections with their own unique perspectives and professional induction experiences as teachers and as professors. After all, it is possible to be a novice several times in different roles with accumulating knowledge and experience (Hughs, Jewson, & Unwin, 2007).

Unfortunately this aspect of linking preservice education and preparation with induction components through university teacher educators' continued contact with novice teachers is frequently without support, scope, or sequence, if it happens at all. Perhaps this is true in part to school and university administrative priorities and financial limitations that may vary widely within and across contexts of those unique learning communities in practice.

School and University Administrators: Enhance Collaboration and Retention

Both within school contexts and supportive administration were found to be especially significant pertaining to teacher retention (Boyd et al., 2011). Administrators play a key role in orchestrating, implementing, and developing vastly interconnected systems of formal and informal networks that encourage the participation of new and established educators, formal and informal mentors, school and university administrators, university- and school-based teacher educators.

Although it is important that all administrators take responsibility for the development of a new teacher, the role of the building principal is probably the most critical (Portner, 2001). Members actively participate through learning communities in practice to work together and strengthen effective induction support. Research suggests that novice teachers are more likely to remain in the profession based in part on to what degree they ascertain productive peer collaborations based on professional dynamic exchange and shared duties (Pogodzinski, Youngs, Frank, & Belman, 2013) as well as their observation and experience of productive administration and staff interactions (Pogodzinski et al., 2012).

Thus, the core values of learning communities in practice honor classroom teachers as associated teacher educators and build a comprehensive network of induction and professional development services that address the teaching profession as well as the individual teacher as learner. Assisting novice teachers in the induction period may increase the retention of teachers (Mills, Moore, & Keane, 2001). While the profession recognizes that some teachers who are best suited in another career choose to leave, those teachers who are effective in teaching students are more likely to continue teaching with induction support.

Learning Communities in Practice to Enhance Collaboration and Retention: Implications for Professional Development Organizations

Those teachers who do participate in induction and do not remain teaching as effective teachers cause a financial burden on the school as well as other negative impacts as a result of frequent teacher turn-over (Ingersoll & Strong, 2011). Supportive collaboration is vital for novice teachers' continued learning to teach and remain in the profession.

More discreet support for those who desire to be anonymous in their quest may be found through online assistance that also covers vast distances and is always readily available (Buchanan et al., 2013). Without induction into thriving communities of learners in practice the novice is more likely to stagnate, isolate, and consequently choose to exit the teaching profession.

Induction into learning communities in practice for the novice brings copious advantages for additional learning in the contexts of existing and developing structures of informed values as evident in customs and terminology (Schon, 1987). In the absence of inductive enculturation into the profession in general and the immediate educational environment in particular, individuals may experience varied measures of isolation and lack interconnectedness to the school's intrinsic social systems.

Isolation may be even more intensified for novice special education teachers who usually number only a few of the teaching staff. One significant factor is the location of the novice special education teacher's classroom, which is often remote, the back room, an old computer room, in the basement, outside the building, in a mobile unit, and so on. The location of the novice special education teacher's classroom can hinders collaboration (Youngs et al., 2011).

Reducing isolation is critical as professionals learn from peers. Opportunities for frequent and extensive collaboration are essential to classroom teachers as associated teacher educators. Veteran teachers learn new ideas from novice teachers. Novice teachers benefit from the experienced knowledge of more seasoned educators. Novice special education teachers depend on collegial connectivity with general educators and may frequently initiate this process in order to obtain needed information.

In smaller schools, the novice may express a need to collaborate that extends more readily to teachers in other schools (Hardy, 2012). Special education teachers offer expertise to other teachers, including regular education teachers in terms of teaching students who may require more individualized instruction. The interdependent learning from peers forms a vital core of learning communities in practice that strengthens all induction components (Flores, 2010). Induction centers on professional collaboration that reduces isolation and increases the retention of effective educators.

Collaborative efforts of learning communities in practice do not afford isolation for even one member. Therefore, all teachers as learners and levels as well as contexts of teaching and of learning thrive from connection to learn from one another. Otherwise resources may be utilized in a manner that only serves to reach and teach a select few. Professional development organizations have the potential to link education professionals with resources in ways to benefit the greatest learning for the most learners by building a supportive framework of collaboration between teachers, administrators, and teacher educators as well as higher education institutions.

Collaboration of this magnitude would build links of learning communities in practice and therefore greatly increase the retention of effective education professionals. This includes administrators as well as teachers as associated teacher educators. From such diverse and extensive collaborations of learning communities in practice the support of mentors would also be enhanced.

Areas of further consideration and research include the following:

- In what ways are collaborations of teacher educators, administrators, and teacher enhanced in learning communities in practice?
- How do enhanced collaborations across contexts impact retention?
- What are areas of collaboration and retention best served with the assistance of professional development organizations from the perspectives of teachers, administrators, and teacher educators as well as from the vantage point of the professional development organizations themselves?
- In what ways might professional development organizations strengthen communities of learning in practice to better support mentoring programs?

LEARNING COMMUNITIES IN PRACTICE: MENTORING AND INDUCTION

Often the first teachers the novice may meet in the setting of their first teaching assignment are within close classroom proximity. Administrators may choose to place a novice in a given location to encourage mentoring relationships. Mentoring is viewed as a critical responsibility for all leaders (Sweeny, 2001). Some other teachers may be introduced perhaps through additional common elements experienced such as content taught, grade level, a special needs consult, or other variables within the first few days, weeks, and years of teaching.

Those seemingly casual encounters may have far-reaching consequences for the novice and veteran on the learning to teach continuum. From the internal workings of the social fabric that in part forms communities of learning in practice some more seasoned professionals tend to naturally emerge as informal mentors. Informal mentors are not assigned, and the mentoring relationships develop as certain veteran professionals are identified by the novice as approachably available for ideas and support.

Novices tend to gravitate toward certain individuals through proximity, availability, personality, information, and resources needed. These characteristics of self-selecting a mentor carry over into all levels of education, meaning that they apply to the 1st-grade teacher and the novice assistant professor.

However, mentors who involve novices in the initial conversation set a positive tone and expectation for active engagement for the entire relationship (Zachary, 2000). Therefore, mentors need to take the first step to create a collaborative, colleague-to-colleague learning interchange of professional discourse (Denmark & Podsen, 2000).

While the profession strives to recognize mentoring teachers at the elementary and secondary levels, there is also a need for mentoring K-12 administrators as well as professors in postsecondary institutions. In higher education settings, mentoring relationships are most effective when tailored to the individual novice who chooses his or her mentor (Bell & Treleaven, 2011). The characteristics of certain mentors may be subtle or magnified to the novice.

It is the unique novice and mentor combination that carries the greatest potential into the mentored learning to teach discourse to influence professional development through practice. Yet, common distinctive attributes do generally distinguish mentors from their peers.

Mentors defined. Mentors are defined in part as reflective practitioners with knowledge of school, district, subject matter, and resources (Luft et al., 2010). A mentor is preferably open to the beliefs and potential skills of the new teacher and thus fosters an environment in which the skills can be refined (Peterson & Williams, 1998). The qualities attributed to formal mentors can be just as evident in informal mentors (Tillman, 2000).

Furthermore, mentors are professionals who support individual novices as learners in unique contexts. These multiple situations include varied degrees of certain elements such as learning experiences in preparation programs, school district induction, and continued professional development.

Of course, novice teachers will also naturally find comfort in the company of other novice teachers in further learning to apply what they gleaned in their teacher education and experience. Simultaneously, novice teachers will seek mentored learning to teach in order to compensate for areas they perceive as lacking in their preparation that burdens them even further in the setting where they now teach.

Formal and informal mentors. In addition to informal mentors, formal mentors, those mentors assigned to novice teachers, often have some instruction in mentoring and are also an invaluable resource for induction and beyond. Appropriate training for mentors' expanded teaching role improves the quality of a mentoring program (Holloway, 2001). In addition to training, mentors benefit from continuous professional development and supports offered through learning communities in practice, school university collaborations, or discourse with experienced mentors.

The ongoing support system of induction for mentors serves to aide with the transformation to mentor teacher in a more formal sense of the term (Shillingstad, McGlamery, Davis, & Gilles, 2015). Formal mentors as well as informal mentors may find their time limited that they can devote to mentoring. Consequently, proximity is significant as a quick question can be answered, and opportunities for frequent discourse are increased. Time to meet daily leads to enriched mentoring exchanges (Polikoff, Desimone, Porter, & Hochberg, 2015). Some formal mentors are provided release time to more fully assist novice teachers.

The various pathways in availability and degree of formality mentoring programs assume may be designed and implemented to fit the individual novice, mentor, and school. Further modifications of mentoring occur within each mentor and novice relationship. Nonetheless, formal and informal mentoring serves a critical importance in adequately addressing individual induction needs.

Induction should be an integral part of a larger plan so that mentors and novices are involved in a seamless continuum of professional growth (McKenna, 1998). Furthermore, mentoring serves as a career-long professional development tool; the benefits of mentoring to veteran teachers and school cultures may be as important as those derived by novices (William & Bowman, 2000). Formal and informal mentors along with other members of learning communities in practice form a vital core of induction support for the novice while simultaneously and subsequently benefiting the mentors themselves and others in learning from the professional development process.

The benefits of informal and formal mentoring in the novice teacher's immediate instructional environment are vast. The greatest gift a mentor can give novices is to demonstrate authenticity and realness (Bell, 1997). However, of equal importance are the further learning to teach opportunities brought by colleagues, administrators, university teacher educators, and other professionals in the current and extended educational setting. The school's entire faculty and staff should understand how a mentor program fits with other forms of professional development (Ganser, 2001).

These aspects of learning communities in practice expand and enrich induction experiences in general as well as in content-specific domain areas such as the instruction of writing. However, what induction looks like in one school may be starkly different from another. Mentoring does not occur in a vacuum but within the larger school context (Newcombe, 1988).

While schools and school districts often make a genuine effort to provide induction, they may be deficient in the resources derived from further connections outside of their immediate circles. Induction programs and experiences would benefit from knowing more about what goes on in other schools, districts, states, and countries. A pivotal and far-reaching vehicle for identifying, linking, and implementing as well as evaluating the effects of available resources and ideas from one school to others may serve to greatly enhance induction efforts and results. Hence, mentoring, formal and informal, is another component of induction that stands to be better served through broad-based, well-distributed resources, knowledge, and skills of professional development organizations.

MENTORING: IMPLICATIONS FOR PROFESSIONAL DEVELOPMENT ORGANIZATIONS

Professional development organizations hold the pivotal platform to bring together ideas, substance, and teachers of mentoring in general, as well as in content areas, within and across schools and universities from a local and global perspective. Therefore, professional development organizations may provide information about and deliver services for the renewal of mentoring as a component of teacher induction.

The framework of professional development organizations links schools, teachers, administrators, universities, and higher education teachers to benefit all concerned. To that end, mentoring as a component of induction enhances the professional development of veteran teachers, higher education teachers, as well as school and university administrators in the process, thereby potentially increasing individual student learning in a global context. Learning communities in practice recognize the value of induction for all education professionals, including university teacher educators.

Areas for further consideration and research include the following:

- How might the services of professional development organizations impact mentoring concerning the learning communities in practice in that regard? Specifically, how might mentors across contexts and circumstances connect to share ideas and resources?
- In what ways are mentoring programs for novice teachers, administrators, and higher education novices similar as learning communities in practice? How are the learning communities in practice concerning mentoring different from the perspectives of novice teachers, novice administrators, and novice teacher educators?
- What do experienced mentors, teachers, and administrators see as the role of professional development organizations in best serving mentoring programs at each level of education?

LEARNING COMMUNITIES IN PRACTICE AND INDUCTION: IMPLICATIONS FOR PROFESSIONAL DEVELOPMENT ORGANIZATIONS

Professional development organizations with their pivotal position are more apt to identify common areas of concern as well as goals and objectives between schools and universities, teachers and administrators, university faculty and veteran teachers to foster cohesive opportunities for meaningful exchange. Professional development organizations stand to offer the tremendous potential in the multidimensional aspects of discovering, organizing, and coordinating available local, state, national, and international perspectives, resources, and services to develop and enrich learning communities in practice to the forefront of induction.

Professional development organizations are poised to reach across the situational contexts of K-12 schools' and higher education institutions' offices and classrooms to bring educators of all levels together to share ideas, resources, and support. This is not limited to teachers. The benefits reach all members, and they each are instrumental in creating and sustaining the learning communities in practice (Wiseman et al., 2013).

Administration will grow and learn from other administrators themselves in the midst of their own induction experiences while attempting to support the induction of their staff. University teacher educators will also have much to learn and share with their peers who may also be novices. All of the induction support of administrators and university teacher educators as novices and beyond benefits the teacher induction program in a progressive upward spiral and outward expansion of improved professional development of classroom teachers as associated teacher educators.

The key concepts in this chapter build an adaptable framework of professional development that defines learning communities in practice. This framework is presented in the seven components that follow. However, it is most essential to note that the order is not sequential and each element interacts with the others in multiple capacities based on the unique circumstances of the individual learner and teacher therein.

1. Learning communities in practice consider the individual learning needs of each teacher as learner as well as all learners in this regard.
2. Learning communities in practice share resources and foster mutual growth for other learning communities across international, national, local, and individual contexts through common needs as well as individual differences to continuously support learning, learning to teach, and teaching.
3. Learning communities in practice provide opportunities and share resources for connecting with peers as well as those with more experience within and across settings, including an integration of learning communities in practice around the world and across the nation to break down barriers, reduce isolation, and promote learning at all levels to improve student learning and teacher retention.

4. Learning communities in practice incorporate an internal and external system that continuously assesses the effectiveness of their efforts and incorporates the voices to represent all teachers as learners and learners at all levels.
5. Learning communities in practice informally and formally visit at least annually the individual goals and objectives with feedback from peers and others who contribute to individual teacher and learner growth, including self-assessments.
6. Learning communities in practice include the integration of higher education into the classrooms of K-12 teachers as teacher educators in the field and in connection to classroom teachers collaborating with university teacher educators and professional development opportunities both on and off campus for enrichment of peer learning opportunities.
7. Learning communities in practice bring together numerous communities of practice from all levels of education to share ideas, concerns, and resources in support of professional development through induction and beyond.

Teachers' needs in this regard are to be noted and their desired professional development opportunities be made available to the greatest possible extent. Teachers, teacher educators, and administrators are instrumental in opening the door to invite, cultivate, and grow communities of teachers as learners that seek to reduce isolation and create the purposeful practice of collaboration.

Obviously the implications for professional development organizations are vast. Professional development organizations are called to the challenge to assist in establishing and further developing communities of learning in practice that support classroom teachers as associated teacher educators in induction and throughout the learning to teach continuum.

Learning Communities in Practice and Professional Development Organizations: A Global Perspective

These induction components will incorporate a strong framework that begins building from the existing climate, culture, and contexts of a teacher in a school (Feiman-Nemser, 2010; Flores, 2010; Smith & Finch, 2010). This application is as specific as an individual teacher's induction of writing or as broad as linking international induction efforts to improve learning, teaching, and learning to teach in local, state, national, and international realms.

This is illustrated in China's "model of interlocking teacher networks," which defines in part professional learning communities through internal and external teacher collaboration. This may have useful implications in the

"United States where professional learning communities and teacher networks are still just emerging innovations themselves" (Sargent, 2015, p. 127).

A full global teacher induction investigation of the professional research literature is in order to learn the many benefits of additional approaches in contexts relative to current and future induction programs and associated communities of learning in practice. Further research is required concerning the multiple dimensions of all areas of higher education in addition to teacher education (Martinez, 2008).

The purposeful direction of professional development organizations stands to uphold and expand learning communities in practice on all levels of schools and situations with classroom teachers as associated teacher educators. This vast networking system when utilized to potential will link invaluable opportunities for extensive multilevel teacher collaboration to strengthen and redefine induction for the education profession within locally immediate as well as globally extensive frameworks.

REFERENCES

Association of Teacher Educators' Standards for Teacher Educators. Retrieved from http://www.ate1.org/pubs/uploads/tchredstds0308.pdf

Bausmith, J.M., & Barry, C. (2011). Revisiting professional learning communities to increase college readiness: The importance of pedagogical content knowledge. *Educational Researcher, 40*(4), 175–178.

Bell, A., & Treleaven, L. (2011). Looking for professor right: Mentee selection of mentors in a formal mentoring program. *Higher Education, 61*(5), 545–561.

Bell, C.R. (1997). The bluebird's secret: Mentoring with bravery and balance. *Training and Development,* 5, 30–33.

Bergeron, B.S. (2008). Enacting a culturally responsive curriculum in a novice teacher's classroom. *Urban Education 43*(1), 4–28.

Billett, S. (2007). Including the missing subject: Placing the personal within the community. In J. Hughes, N. Jewson, & L. Unwin (Eds.), *Communities of practice critical perspectives* (pp. 55–67). New York, NY: Routledge.

Bishop, A.G., Brownell, M.T., Klingner, J.K., Leko, M.M., & Galman, S.A.C. (2010). Differences in beginning special education teachers: The influence of personal attributes, preparation, and school environment on classroom reading. *Learning Disability Quarterly, 33*(2), 75–92.

Bodger, C.L. (2011). *Novice principals' perceptions of beginning principal support and induction* (Doctoral dissertation). Retrieved from ProQuest (3472519).

Borko, H. (2004). Professional development and teacher learning: Mapping the terrain. *Educational Researcher, 33*(8), 3–15.

Boyd, D., Grossman, P., Ing, M., Lankford, H., Loeb. S., & Wyckoff, J. (2011). The influence of school administration on teacher retention decisions. *American Educational Research Association, 48*(2), 303–333.

Buchanan, J., Prescott, A., Schuck, S., Aubusson, P., Burke, P., & Louviere, J. (2013). Teacher retention and attrition: Views of early career teachers. *Australian Journal of Teacher Education, 38*(3), 110–129.

Chubbick, S.M., Clift, R.T., Allard, J., & Quinlan, J. (2001). Playing it safe as a novice teacher: Implications for programs for new teachers. *Journal of Teacher Education, 52*(5), 365–376.

Cuban, L. (1993). *How teachers taught: Constancy and change in American Classrooms, 1890–1990* (2nd ed.). New York, NY: Teachers College Press.

Denmark, V.M., & Podsen, I.J. (2000). The mettle of a mentor. *Journal of Staff Development, 21*(4), 18–22.

Feiman-Nemser, S. (2001). From preparation to practice: Designing a continuum to strengthen and sustain teaching. *Teachers College Record, 103*(6), 1013–1055.

Feiman-Nemser, S. (2010). Multiple meanings of new teacher induction. In J. Wang, S.J. Odell, & R.T. Clift (Eds.), *Past, present, and future research on teacher induction* (pp. 15–30). Lanham, MD: Rowman & Littlefield Publishers, Inc.

Flores, M.A. (2010). School cultures and organizations and teacher induction. In J. Wang, S.J. Odell, & R.T. Clift (Eds.), *Past, present, and future research on teacher induction,* (pp. 45–56). Lanham, MD: Rowman & Littlefield Publishers, Inc.

Freiberg, M.R. (2000). Coaching and mentoring first-year and student teachers. *NASSP Bulletin, 84,* 87–88.

Ganser, T. (1999). The principal as new teacher mentor. *Journal of Staff Development, 22*(1), 39–41.

Gilbert, J., & Graham, S. (2010). Teaching writing to elementary students in grades 4–6: A national survey. *The Elementary School Journal, 110*(4), 494–518.

Goodlad, J.I. (2004). The guiding mission. In J.I. Goodlad & T.J. McManon (Eds.), *The teaching career* (pp. 19–46). New York, NY: Columbia University: Teachers College Press.

Graves, D.H. (2002). *Testing is not teaching.* Portsmouth, NH: Heinemann.

Hammerness, K., Darling-Hammond, L., Bransford, J., Berliner, D., Cochran-Smith, M., McDonald, M., & Zeichner, K. (2005). How teachers learn and develop. In L. Darling- Hammond & J. Bransford (Eds.), *Preparing teachers for a changing world* (pp. 358–389). San Francisco, CA: Jossey-Bass.

Hardy, S.L. (2012). *Constructing exemplary practice in the teaching of writing and professional English language arts standards: Implications for novice special education teachers* (Doctoral dissertation).

Hargreaves, A. & Fullan, M. (2000). Mentoring in the new millennium. *Theory into Practice, 39*(1), 50–56.

Henry, G.T., Bastian, K.C., & Fortner, C.K. (2011). Stayers and leavers: Early career teacher effectiveness and attrition. *Educational Researcher, 40*(6), 271–280.

Hollway, J.H. (2001). The benefits of mentoring. *Educational Leadership, 58*(8), 85–86.

Hughes, J., Jewson, N., & Unwin, L. (2007). Conclusion, further developments and unresolved issues. In J. Hughes, N. Jewson, & L. Unwin (Eds.), *Communities of practice critical perspectives* (pp. 171–176). New York, NY: Routledge.

Ingersoll, R.M., & Strong, M. (2011). The impact of induction and mentoring programs for beginning teachers: A critical review of the research. *Review of Educational Research, 81*(2), 201–233.

Ingersoll, R.M., Merrill, L., & May, H. (2014). *What are the effects of teacher education and preparation on beginning teacher attrition?* Research Report (#RR-82). Philadelphia: Consortium for Policy Research in Education, University of Pennsylvania.

Iordandides, G., & Vyroni, M. (2013). School leaders and the induction of new teachers. *International Studies in Educational Administration 41*(1), 75–88.

James, N. (2007). The learning trajectories of "old-timers": Academic identities and communities of practice in higher education. In J. Hughes, N. Jewson, & L. Unwin (Eds.), *Communities of practice critical perspectives* (pp. 131–143). New York, NY: Routledge.

Johnson, S.M. (2015). Will VAMS reinforce the walls of the egg-crate school? *Educational Researcher, 44*(2), 117–123.

Johnson, S.M., Kraft, M., & Papay, J.P. (2012). How context matters in high-need schools: The effects of teachers' working conditions on their professional satisfaction and their students' achievement. *Teachers College Record, 114*(10), 1–39.

Kagan, D.M. (1992). Professional growth among pre-service and beginning teachers. *Review of Educational Research, 62*(2), 129–169.

Kiuhara, S.A., Hawken, L.S., & Graham, S. (2009). Teaching writing to high school students: A national survey. *Journal of Educational Psychology, 101*(1), 136–160.

Knowles, J.G., & Cole, A.L. (2015). We're just like the beginning teachers we study: Letters and reflections on our first year as beginning professors. *Curriculum Inquiry, 24*(1), 27–52.

Lave, J., & Wenger, E. (2015). *Situated learning legitimate peripheral participation.* Chelsea, MI: Sheridan Books, Inc.

Luft, J.A., Neakrase, J.J., Adams, K.L., & Bang, E. (2010). Bringing content into induction programs. In J. Wang, S.J. Odell, & R.T. Clift (Eds.), *Past, present, and future research on teacher induction* (pp. 205–220). Lanham, MD: Rowman & Littlefield Publishers, Inc.

Martinez, K. (2008). Academic induction for teacher educators. *Asia-Pacific Journal of Teacher Education, 36*(1), 35–51.

Massey, D.D. (2006). "You teach for me; I've had it!" A first-year teacher's cry for help. *Action in Teacher Education, 28*(3), 7–85.

McKenna, G. (1998). Mentor training: The key to effective staff development. *Principal, 77,* 47–49.

Mills, H., Moore, D., & Keane, G.W. (2001). Addressing the teacher shortage: A study of successful mentoring programs in Oakland County, Michigan. *The Clearing House, 74,* 124–126.

Moir, E., & Gless, J. (2001). Quarterly induction: An investment in teachers. *Teacher Education Quarterly, 28*(1), 109–114.

Murray, J. (2005). Readdressing the priorities: New teacher educators and induction into higher education. *European Journal of Teacher Education, 28(1),* 67–85.

Newcombe, E. (1988). *Mentoring programs for new teachers.* Philadelphia, PA: Research for Better Schools.

Palincsar, A.S. (1998). Social constructivist perspectives on teaching and learning. *Annual Review of Psychology, 49,* 345–375.

Pardo, L.S. (2006). The role of contexts in learning to teach writing. *Journal of Teacher Education, 57*(4), 378–394.

Peterson, B.E., & Williams, S.R. (1998). Mentoring beginning teachers. *Mathematics Teachers, 91*(8), 730–734.

Pogodzinski, B., Youngs, P., Frank, K.A., & Belman, D. (2012). Administrative climate and novices' intent to remain teaching. *The Elementary School Journal, 113*(2), 252–275.

Polikoff, M.S., Desimone, L.M., Porter, A.C., & Hochberg, E.D. (2015). Mentor policy and the quality of mentoring. *The Elementary School Journal, 116*(1), 76–102.

Portner, H. (2001). *Training mentors is not enough, everything else schools and districts need to do*. Thousand Oaks, CA: Corwin Press, Inc.

Prather-Jones, B. (2011). How administrators influence the retention of teachers of students with emotional and behavioral disorders. *Clearing House, 84*, 1–8.

Putnam, R.T., & Borko, H. (2000). What do new views of knowledge and thinking have to say about research on teacher learning? *Educational Researcher, 29*(1), 4–15.

Sargent, T.C. (2015). Professional learning communities and the diffusion of pedagogical innovation in the Chinese education system. *Comparative Education Review, 59*(1), 102–132.

Schmidt, W.H., Burroughs, N.A., Zoido, P., & Houang, R.T. (2015). The role of schooling in perpetuating educational inequality: An international perspective. *Educational Researcher, 44*(7), 371–383.

Schon, (1987). *Educating the reflective practitioner*. San Francisco, CA: Jossey-Bass Publishers.

Schillingstad, S.L., McGlamery, S., Davis, B., & Giles, C. (2015). Navigating the roles of leadership: Mentors' perspectives on teacher leadership. *The Delta Kappa Gamma Bulletin,* winter, 12–30.

Shulman, L.S. (1986). Those who understand: Knowledge growth in teaching. *Educational Researcher, 15*(2), 4–14.

Smith (2007). How do state-level induction and standards-based reform policies affect induction experiences and turnover among new teachers? *American Journal of Education, 113*, 273–309.

Smith, T.M., & Finch, M. (2010). Influence of teacher induction on teacher retention. In J. Wang, S.J. Odell, & R.T. Clift (Eds.), *Past, present, and future research on teacher induction* (pp. 109–124). Lanham, MD: Rowman & Littlefield Publishers, Inc.

Sullivan, S., & Glanz, J. (2000). Alternative approaches to supervision: Cases from the field. *Journal of Curriculum and Supervision, 15*(3), 212–235.

Swanson, P.B. (2010). Teacher efficacy and attrition: Helping students at the introductory levels of language instruction appears critical. *American Association of Teachers of Spanish and Portuguese, 93*(2), 305–321.

Sweeny, B. (2001). *Taking a closer look: Best practices for continuous, high impact teacher development*. Wheaton, IL: Best Practice Resources.

Tillman, B.A. (2000). Quiet leadership: informal mentoring of beginning teachers. *Momentum, 31*(1), 24–26.

Troia, G., & Maddox, M. (2004). Writing instruction in middle schools: Special and general education teachers share their views and voice their concerns. *Exceptionality, 12*(1), 19–37.

Wenger, E. (2008). *Communities of practice,* New York, NY: Cambridge University Press.

Wideen, M., Mayer-Smith, J., & Moon, B. (1998). A critical analysis of the research on learning to teach: Making the case for an ecological perspective on inquiry. *Review of Educational Research, 68*(2), 130–178.

Williams, D.A., & Bowman, C.L. (2000). Reshaping the professions one teacher at a time. Collaborative mentoring of entry year teachers, In J. McIntyre & D. Byrd (Eds.), *Research on effective models of teacher education* (pp. 173–187). Thousand Oaks, CA: Corwin Press, Inc.

Wiseman, P., Arroyo, H., & Richter, N. (2013). *Reviving professional learning communities*, London: Rowman & Littlefield Publishers, Inc.

Wisniewski, R, (2004). Today is tomorrow. In J.I. Goodlad & T.J. McMannon (Eds.), *The teaching career* (pp. 184–210). New York, NY: Columbia University, Teachers College Press.

Wood, A.L. (2005). The importance of principals: Site administrators' roles in novice teacher induction. *American Secondary Education, 33*(2), 39–62.

Youngs, P., Jones, N., & Low, M. (2011). How beginning special and general education elementary teachers negotiate role expectations and access professional resources. *Teachers College Record, 113*(7), 1506–1540.

Zachary, L.J. (2000). *The mentor's guide*. San Francisco, CA: Jossey-Bass.

Zeichner, K., Tabachnick, B.R., & Densmore, K. (1987). Individual, institutional, and cultural influences on the development of teachers' craft knowledge. In J. Calderhead (Ed.), *Exploring teachers' thinking* (pp. 1–20). Eastbourne, England: Cassell.

Chapter Two

Qualities of Effective Teacher Leaders

Meagan Musselman, Lynn Gannon Patterson, and Greg Gierhart

ABSTRACT

This chapter analyzes some of the qualities effective teacher leaders possess, including utilizing a professional vision, implementing co-teaching strategies, providing and participating in continuous professional development, engaging in professional dialogue, partnering with families, participating in professional communities, and showing professionalism. Qualities are examined through the lens of different teaching and leadership frameworks, such as Danielson's Framework for Teaching. In addition, this chapter explores strategies for building a culture of leadership capacity that will support the growth of teachers as leaders.

KEYWORDS

Associated teacher educator, Framework for Teaching, leadership capacity, professional dialogue, professional vision, teacher leadership

INTRODUCTION

Teacher leadership encompasses a broad view of the roles and responsibilities teachers take upon themselves to impact the educational outcomes of not only the students in their classrooms but also those students in other teachers' classrooms. One of those roles involves serving as associated teacher educators focused on helping preservice and novice teachers become more proficient in the field of education. Because preservice and novice teachers naturally lack the hands-on experience and expertise of veteran teachers, they can benefit greatly from teacher leaders who are willing to model, co-teach, and provide other support.

Increasingly, graduate programs in education are promoting the development of teacher leadership. Carver and Meier (2013) drew upon the written reflections of early career teachers in their study on early career conceptions of teacher leadership during graduate coursework.

They reported several examples that illustrated ways in which early career teachers' thinking might be evolving regarding teacher leadership: Although teachers' conceptualizations of leadership seemed to be expanding, teachers still had a sense of their personal investment in leadership; early career teachers defined teacher leadership as not simply the privilege of formally designated leaders but something for which all teachers should strive; and, teachers acknowledged that a lack of time and expertise inhibited their propensity to assume great leadership responsibility.

The authors also uncovered factors that limited early career teachers' interest in teacher leadership, including concerns with gaining expertise and confidence, fear and uncertainty about their roles, and fear of asking an experienced colleague for help. Roughly half of the study's participants reported working in settings where fellow teachers acted as obstacles to their learning and leadership. Carver and Meier's findings highlight both the promise and the challenge of preparing early career teachers for a range of leadership roles and responsibilities.

Riveros, Newton, and da Costa (2013) conducted a study on teacher leadership in which they interviewed 21 teachers and administrators about their experiences in a provincial teacher-leader program from 1997 to 2007. They found that the path to teacher leadership encompassed four themes: (a) teacher leaders tend to arise through informal leadership processes in their schools and districts; (b) teacher leaders cultivate a broader understanding of educational leadership when they work across school contexts, such as moving beyond the classroom teaching role and embracing innovative practices like professional collaboration with others; (c) teacher leaders can be recruited into leadership roles by focusing on their professional interests and passions; and (d) teacher leaders need flexible school structures that facilitate trust and cooperation with their peers.

Because teacher leaders can serve an important role as associated teacher educators in support of both preservice and novice teachers, it is important to identify the qualities of effective teacher leaders. These qualities include the following: (a) utilizing a professional vision, (b) implementing co-teaching strategies, (c) providing and participating in continuous professional development, (d) engaging in professional dialogue, (e) partnering with families, (f) participating in professional communities, and (g) showing professionalism.

However, it is important to keep in mind that teacher leadership is effective only if a school creates a culture that builds leadership capacity where teacher leaders can thrive. Thus, this chapter will focus on examining each of the qualities of teacher leaders through the lens of different teaching and leadership frameworks, followed by a discussion on strategies for building a culture of leadership capacity that will support the growth of teachers as leaders.

TEACHER LEADER QUALITIES

Utilizing a Professional Vision

Kentucky recently released a draft of the Kentucky Teacher Leadership Framework (Kentucky Teacher Leadership Work Team, 2015), which utilizes Charles Goodwin's (1994) notion of *professional vision* as a basis. This framework is grounded in the idea that teacher leaders need to work together to create a professional vision that highlights features of effective pedagogical practice that will improve the profession. They must also be able to effectively communicate that professional vision in order to affect change, innovation, and reform. Decision makers outside of the classroom might not understand the professional vision and would therefore need the teacher leaders to identify and explain the intricate details of effective or ineffective pedagogical practices and suggestions for improvement.

Teacher leadership is often difficult to define because of the many facets of leadership it encompasses. As reflected in Kentucky's framework, there are multiple roles a teacher leader fills in order to positively enhance student learning; these roles span from the classroom to working with colleagues to influencing the profession as a whole.

More specifically, the Kentucky Teacher Leadership Framework is composed of six dimensions, each of which focuses on a role that teacher leaders might take on: Leading From the Classroom: Developing Capacities of Student and Self; Leading Through Modeling and Coaching: Developing

Capacities of Peers; Leading Groups and Teams: Contributing to Positive School Change to Enhance Student Learning; Leading to Increase Teacher Voice and Influence: Working to Enlarge Teachers' Role in Decision-Making Beyond the Classroom and in Concert With Other Stakeholders; Leading to Professionalize Teaching: Reforming Educational Systems to Create Greater Opportunities for Teachers to Learn and Lead Beyond the Local Level; and Leading to Connect to the Larger Community or World: Expanding the World of the Classroom Beyond the School.

In the framework document, the description of each dimension includes (a) an overview of the leadership role, (b) a vignette, (c) a list of core beliefs about the type of leadership, (d) dispositions expected from the type of leadership, and (e) the knowledge and skills necessary for the type of leadership (Kentucky Teacher Leadership Work Team, 2015).

Through the use of a professional vision, teachers can become effective instructional leaders. According to Mangin and Stoelinga (2009), "Instructional teacher leaders commonly perform an array of activities: conduct professional development workshops, co-plan and model lessons, observe teaching and provide feedback, collect and analyze data, facilitate dialogue and reflective critique, and promote shared practices among peers" (p. 49).

As instructional teacher leaders, they verbalize the details of instructional design and delivery through their developed professional vision. Novice teachers are able to develop their own professional vision through dialogue with these instructional teacher leaders in a nonsupervisory environment.

Implementing Co-Teaching Strategies

Co-teaching has frequently been utilized in the special education domain for a number of years as a way to achieve full inclusion of special education students in a mainstream classroom (Cook & Friend, 1995). St. Cloud University has led the way in utilizing co-teaching as an effective way for student teachers to collaborate with classroom teachers and has evidence to suggest it enhances student achievement (Bacharach, Heck, & Dahlberg, 2010).

In St. Cloud's model of a co-taught classroom, the cooperating teacher (classroom teacher) is a teacher leader and an associated teacher educator through the involvement with and teaching of the student teacher. In this model, both teachers (the cooperating teacher and student teacher) work together to remain actively involved in student learning rather than using a tag-team approach where one is teaching while the other is doing something else.

In a more traditional model of student teaching that might be viewed as a "sink or swim" experience, the expertise of the cooperating teacher is often untapped. A novice teacher leads instruction without the proper guidance of the veteran teacher. In St. Cloud's co-teaching model, the cooperating teacher provides ongoing modeling and coaching. These teacher leaders help develop the professional vision for the student teacher by making the invisible visible via explicitly sharing their rationale for instructional, management, or assessment decisions (Bacharach et al., 2010).

Serving as an associated teacher educator through the role of a cooperating teacher with a student teacher is a critical way for teacher leaders to contribute to the profession. Preservice teachers learn a variety of curricula, instructional strategies, behavior management techniques, and assessments in their teacher training programs but need the guidance and expertise of a cooperating teacher to coach them into successful implementation.

Teacher leaders' willingness to co-teach aligns with Standard 1 of the Association of Teacher Educators' (2008) *Standards for Teacher Educators*, which stipulates that accomplished teacher educators model effective instruction. Teacher leaders who are willing to co-teach can exhibit this standard by demonstrating and promoting effective teaching practices and classroom management with novice teachers.

Providing and Participating in Continuous Professional Development

Over 15 years ago, Barth (2001) argued that all teachers have the capacity to lead their schools down a more positive path and to use their abundant experience to craft knowledge in the service of school improvement. Those experiences are gathered and processed through professional development garnered from a variety of sources, including entering graduate programs, participating in district- and state-level trainings, attending and presenting at professional conferences, seeking additional certifications or degrees, and more. Lambert (2003) noted that professional development is particularly important in student learning because it shapes teacher beliefs, assumptions, and practice.

Charlotte Danielson's (2008) Framework for Teaching, which is a comprehensive framework focused on the specific aspects of a teacher's responsibilities that have been proven through research to promote improved student learning, includes a component—Domain 4: Professional Responsibilities—that emphasizes the importance of professional development for effective teacher leaders.

The framework includes performance descriptors for teacher leaders, ranging from *unsatisfactory* to *distinguished*, and Standard 4e: Growing and Developing Professionally states that a distinguished teacher leader "actively pursues professional development opportunities and initiates activities to contribute to the profession" (p. 135).

In addition, Standard 4e notes that a distinguished teacher leader "seeks feedback from supervisors and colleagues" (p. 135). Teacher leaders understand the value of constructive feedback from supervisors and colleagues and take advantage of that feedback to make improvements to their own teaching and learning. All of these experiences help teachers gain instructional confidence in the classroom, manage conflicts with colleagues, and lead instructional improvement.

Teachers' prior knowledge shapes what and how they learn from professional development (PD). Of particular importance is teachers' practical knowledge, that is, knowledge they draw on daily to plan and organize their instruction (vanDriel, 2001). Sometimes, teachers' practical knowledge helps them to interpret ideas and resources from PD, but just as easily, such knowledge can interfere with teachers' making changes intended by leaders of professional development (Kazemi & Hubbard, 2008).

Recent research on teacher PD underscores the importance of the coherence of PD with standards, curriculum, and assessment. Teachers' judgments of the coherence of PD with larger system goals influence their decisions about what ideas and resources they appropriate from PD (Allen & Penuel, 2015).

How teachers systematically reflect upon their practices and how they are committed to the importance of continuous professional development is key to the teacher leader model. In fact, the Association of Teacher Educators' (2008) standard on professional development (Standard 4) states that accomplished teacher educators "inquire systematically into, reflect on, and improve their own practice and demonstrate commitment to continuous professional development" (p. 4).

Along these same lines, Danielson's (2008) Framework for Teaching, Standard 4a: Reflecting on Teaching, states that for a distinguished teacher leader, "The teacher's reflection on the lesson is thoughtful and accurate, citing specific evidence. The teacher draws on an extensive repertoire to suggest alternative strategies and predicts the likely success of each" (p. 134).

This component of reflective practice may include the teacher leader writing about a lesson immediately following it, identifying specific evidence from the lesson by way of professional vision that supports future learning opportunities, and then sharing those reflections with other colleagues to learn from each other. This sharing aspect ties directly to the professional dialogue quality discussed next.

Engaging in Professional Dialogue

It is through involving novice teachers in professional dialogue conversations that teacher leaders are able to serve as associated teacher educators. The face of professional dialogue has changed with new technological medians that allow teachers to easily share their reflections. For instance, a teacher leader today often shares through social media. Teachers are exploring the boundaries of their practice together on Twitter, in blogs, and at on-demand seminars, and they represent a new generation of educators who are actively redefining how innovation occurs in the schoolhouse (Ferriter & Provenzano, 2013).

Of course, this collaboration also includes popular sites like Teachers Pay Teachers and Pinterest. Additionally, educators who have embraced reflecting and sharing in new technological learning spaces often display a passionate commitment to the tools, the process, and their peers. Some have said that they have learned more in shorter periods in their Twitter stream or at Edcamps than in hours of professional development sessions (Ferriter & Provenzano, 2013).

Another standard from Danielson's (2008) Framework for Teaching that supports the need for professional dialogue is Standard 4b: Maintaining Accurate Records. This standard states that a teacher's system for maintaining both instructional and non-instructional records should be accurate, efficient, and effective, and students should contribute to its maintenance. Thus, although it is the teacher leader's professional responsibility to maintain records of progress accurately, efficiently, and effectively, the student voice is essential to meeting the students' instructional learning needs.

The value of student contributions is essential to consider in every classroom situation; after all, teaching is about the students, what they learn, how they respond to the learning, and their engagement. Collecting and gathering student feedback is critical for every teacher leader to move the learning forward. Sources of evidence could include notes from reflection conferences, the teacher's own reflections, reflective debriefings with students, and even teacher interviews.

Despite its importance, the most valuable aspect in Danielson's (2008) Framework for Teaching does not consist of the acquisition of skill in assembling evidence for the different components; instead, the greatest value derives from the professional conversations among educators about their practices. It is through professional dialogues that novice teachers are able to learn best practices from teacher leaders.

These professional dialogues influence the culture of the learning community among teachers and allow a venue for experienced teachers—whether teacher leaders or not—to share experiences and insight with colleagues who are facing dilemmas that they have already faced.

Partnering With Families

Standard 4c: Communicating With Families, from Danielson's (2008) Framework for Teaching, states that for a distinguished teacher leader, "the teacher's communication with families is frequent and sensitive to cultural traditions and students participate in the communication. The teacher successfully engages families in the instructional program, as appropriate" (p. 134).

According to Danielson, methods for communicating with families can include teacher interactions with parents at school events, phone calls, weekly newsletters, and handouts on descriptions of programs. Of course, there are many ways teacher leaders can communicate with families using technology. One example is a popular app called Class Dojo, which allows teachers to send instant messages, photos, announcements, and more to keep students engaged and to communicate with parents.

Communication with families is key to ensuring successful interventions for students as well. For instance, schools that design and implement a Pyramid Response to Intervention program often fail to communicate the system's goals and procedures to students and parents (Buffman, Mattos, & Weber, 2009). The role of the teacher leader is to communicate such information effectively to families and the student.

Additionally, punitive perceptions stem from cases in which students, having been referred for interventions, feel that they are in trouble. Students may already find it stressful to meet with an administrator or counselor regarding insufficient academic achievement. These feelings detract from the goal of developing positive, supportive relationships with students that can help them build confidence and achieve greater success.

For this reason, teacher leaders should discuss with students and parents an intervention's decidedly non-punitive purpose *before* referring a student to an intervention program (Buffman et al., 2009).

Clear communication with all stakeholders is essential to student success. Thus, it is an important responsibility of teacher leaders to share their expertise on effective communication methods with novice teachers.

Participating in Professional Communities

For teacher leaders, participation in a professional community can take many shapes and forms. Teachers can, of course, participate in school events and even attend community events such as ball games, movie night, plays, and academic competitions. Teachers can spend time in professional learning community (PLC) meetings with their colleagues and administrators to reflect, analyze data, debrief, and make important changes.

The basic structure of PLCs involves collaborative teams whose members work interdependently to achieve *common goals*. The team is the engine that drives the PLC effort. Some organizations base their improvement strategies on efforts to enhance the knowledge and skills of individuals; however, even though individual growth is essential for organizational growth to take place, it does not guarantee organizational growth. Building a school's capacity to learn is a collective rather than an individual task. People who engage in collaborative team learning are able to learn from one another and thus create momentum to fuel continued improvement. It is difficult to overstate the importance of collaborative teams in the improvement process (DuFour, DuFour, Eaker, & Karhanek, 2004).

Standard 4d in Danielson's (2008) Framework for Teaching focuses on professional communities and suggests that a distinguished teacher leader "makes substantial contributions to the professional community, to school and district events and projects, and assumes a leadership role among the faculty" (p. 134). In most cases, active participation in professional communities leads to leadership because members have a shared purpose or goal.

Some states have created leadership networks with the intent of building capacity for assessment literacy, better understanding the common core standards, deconstructing the standards into learning targets, and designing high-quality instruction and assessment. Leadership networks extend the professional community of teacher leaders beyond the school or district and allow teachers to collaborate with colleagues from other districts (Kentucky Department of Education, 2015).

Showing Professionalism

Standard 4f: Showing Professionalism, from Danielson's (2008) Framework for Teaching, maintains that the distinguished teacher leader is proactive and assumes a leadership role in making sure that school practices and procedures honor all students, particularly those traditionally underserved. In addition, the teacher displays the highest standards of ethical conduct and takes a leadership role in ensuring that colleagues comply with school and district regulations.

As teachers become more confident in their ability to lead, they will begin to assume more leadership roles within and outside of the school setting. Teachers can lead and conduct team and faculty meetings, or they may serve as a grade-level team leader, a subject-area team leader, or a committee team leader within the school. Teachers may also serve through leadership at the district level on teams that support learning and meeting the needs of students.

This section provided detailed descriptions of research-based qualities of effective teacher leaders. However, as the next section discusses, it is critical to remember that an important contributor to teacher leadership is a culture of inquiry. It is essential that all educators recognize that the work of professional learning never ends; it is a career-long endeavor.

When school leaders (both teachers and administrators) insist that it is part of every teacher's responsibility to engage in professional development, it is not to suggest that teachers, either individually or collectively, are deficient in their practice. Rather, it is to maintain that teaching is so complex that it is never done perfectly; every educator can always become more skilled and more expert, and making a commitment to do so is part of the essential work of teaching. It is not an add-on, an extra; rather, it is integral to that work (Danielson, 2008).

CREATING LEADERSHIP CAPACITY

Teacher leadership is effective only if a school creates a culture that promotes leadership capacity. In an environment that values building leadership capacity, teacher leaders can continually evolve and serve as effective associated teacher educators. Lambert (2003) developed a continuum of emerging teacher leadership focused on the areas of adult development, dialogue, collaboration, and organizational change. For each construct of teacher leadership, she included associated performance standards based on a continuum that advances from "good" to "great." As Jim Collins (2001) pointed out in his book *Good to Great* (2001):

> Good is the enemy of great. And that is one of the key reasons why we have so little that becomes great. We don't have great schools, principally because we have good schools. We don't have great government, principally because we have good government. Few people attain great lives, in large part because it is just so easy to settle for a good life. (p. 1)

Lambert's standards on the continuum model this notion. In each instance, the piece that gets added to the original good standard is the incorporation of others and taking on leadership roles to make it a great standard. Table 2.1 provides examples of the standards that appear on Lambert's continuum of emerging teacher leadership.

When considering the qualities of effective teacher leaders, we must begin with the qualities of effective teachers. It seems unlikely one would be an effective leader of something in which he or she is not yet distinguished. Lambert noted many connections between the qualities of an effective teacher and an effective teacher leader. The "good" column in Table 2.1 lists standards administrators would be pleased for teachers to possess. However, in terms of advancing leadership capacity within a school, the "great" column better describes the qualities administrators would want to see in teachers.

Lambert (2003) defined leadership as "reciprocal, purposeful learning in a community. Reciprocity helps us build relationships of mutual regard, thereby enabling us to become co-learners. And as co-learners we are also co-teachers, engaging each other through our teaching and learning approaches" (p. 2).

Table 2.1. Examples of Moving From Good to Great Along Lambert's Continuum of Emerging Teacher Leadership

From Good...	To Great...
Engages in personal reflection to improve practice. Models improvements for others in the school community. Shares views with others and develops an understanding of others' assumptions.	Evokes reflection in others. Develops and supports a culture of self-reflection that may include collaborative planning, peer coaching, action research, and reflective writing.
Communicates well with individuals and groups in the community as a means to create and sustain relationships and focus on teaching and learning. Actively participates in dialogue.	Facilitates effective dialogue among members of the school community in order to build relationships and focus the dialogue on teaching and learning.
Participates actively in team building. Seeks roles and opportunities to contribute to the team. Sees teamwork as central to the community.	Engages colleagues in team-building activities that develop mutual trust and promote collaborative decision making.

Note. Adapted from *Leadership Capacity for Lasting School Improvement*, by Linda Lambert, 2003, Alexandria, VA: Association for Supervision and Curriculum Development, pp. 103–104. Copyright 2003 by the Association for Supervision and Curriculum Development. Adapted with permission.

There are strong similarities between constructivist teachers and constructivist teacher leaders.

As associated teacher educators, teacher leaders use the same constructs they employ in their classrooms with students, but on a broader scale with novice teachers. Some of the activities teachers use with students that they can also use with novice teachers include modeling, coaching, articulation, and reflection. Lambert also noted that leading and learning are intertwined, and that leading is fundamental to the nature and mission of teaching. Therefore, teachers should naturally progress to become teacher leaders within their schools, districts, and the profession.

Watching an athletic coach build capacity within a team is truly an amazing experience, of which educators should take note. It is magical to see how a coach uses various capacity building techniques to motivate athletes to win games. Take, for example, the book *You Win in the Locker Room First: The 7 C's to Build a Winning Team in Business, Sports, and Life,* by Jon Gordon and Mike Smith (2015).

The authors suggested that capacity building from the athletic field can be used as a best practice in any profession, and thus they created a system to empower readers to build a culture of greatness, which is important in any profession. They suggested that a coach, and thus by extension any effective leader, must (a) develop talent; (b) be optimistic when handling negativity boldly and swiftly; (c) know how to be infectious; (d) be consistent;

and (e) know the importance of communicating, connecting, and making commitments.

All of these traits are connected to how the administrators of the Kentucky Department of Education (2015) envisioned building capacity to implement the sweeping changes involved in the most recent education reform in the Commonwealth of Kentucky, known as Senate Bill 1.

The approach to this new type of capacity building taken by the Kentucky Department of Education (2015) is based on the current research of effective professional development that leads to improved classroom practice, which is different from the previous train-the-trainer model. One of the most important outcomes of building capacity within an educational setting is to engage educators in dialogue to strive for providing the best education a student can receive.

Capacity building through leadership networks is based on the premise that teachers will attend multiple meetings, be presented material that is current and relevant, and have the opportunity to engage in dialogue with colleagues from other schools and districts. These teacher leaders will then take what they have learned to district meetings and professional learning communities to disseminate the most current information available, thus building capacity for learning and leading.

In contrast, in the more traditional train-the-trainer model, teachers attend trainings and workshops so that they can return to their districts and conduct the same exact training with others. Table 2.2 details how the Kentucky Department of Education distinguishes between capacity building and the train-the-trainer model.

Table 2.2. Different Approaches to Professional Development: Capacity Building vs. Train the Trainer

Capacity Building	Train the Trainer
This type of training allows participants in the network to develop skills, increase knowledge, and build capacity.	This type of training allows participants or the trainers to receive materials and knowledge to be passed on directly to other participants.
Participants make connections between what they are learning and the needs in their districts, and then use the knowledge, resources, and tools from the network meetings to develop a plan specific to their district's needs.	Trainers receive a preplanned, often prepackaged, set of materials to be disseminated at trainings in their district without adapting their training to the challenges the district faces.
Work is conducted collaboratively in the networks to create deliverables (learning targets, instructional resources, etc.) related to Kentucky's Core Academic Standards.	Trainers are given the materials that will be used exactly as they were in the training with the teachers in their districts. Typically, participants duplicate rather than create.

Capacity Building	Train the Trainer
District leadership teams customize a plan for ongoing professional learning for their districts. The knowledge and skills they receive from the network are then applied to help teachers improve instructional practices in their classrooms.	Train-the-trainer trainings are scripted for a particular need and may not address the needs of every school, classroom, or teacher in the district.
This kind of training results in a long-term, sustainable model that best lends itself to delivery in PLCs throughout the school year rather than during fixed 6-hour professional development days.	These trainings are often not conducted as job-embedded professional learning but rather as a whole group training to comply with professional development requirements.

Note. Adapted from *Leadership Networks—Deliverables: Capacity Building vs. Train the Trainer*, by Kentucky Department of Transportation, 2015, http://education.ky.gov/school/Pages/Leadership-Networks—Deliverables.aspx. Copyright 2015 by the Kentucky Department of Education. Adapted with permission.

Schools that nurture a culture that values leadership capacity will reap the benefits of teacher leaders serving as effective associated teacher educators with preservice and novice teachers. The approaches presented in this section can serve as effective models for schools seeking to promote leadership capacity building.

CONCLUSION

The qualities of effective teacher leaders are vast, primarily because the roles of teacher leaders are vast. Teacher leaders are one of schools' most valuable assets, but they must be identified and used appropriately in order to impact student achievement, innovation, and reform. A common problem administrators face with utilizing teacher leaders is that because these individuals are effective classroom teachers, administrators do not want to pull them from the classroom.

Thus, the teacher leaders remain teaching their regular load, and any extra efforts that are willing to make toward leading within the school, district, or profession become additional duties. A creative alternative to this problem is creating hybrid teacher leaders. Hybrid teacher leaders spend about half of their time teaching and instructing students, and the other half of their time coaching, supporting, and modeling effective instruction for novice teachers (Margolis & Huggins, 2012).

This is a great way to ensure that novice teachers learn from the best. The most effective teachers are identified, and through creative scheduling, they are allowed to share their expertise as associated teacher educators with novice teachers.

Teacher leaders have a strong sense of purpose, develop collegial relationships and collaborations, move beyond the boundaries of their classrooms, and influence colleagues without the use of overt power (Riveros et al., 2013). Moving beyond the boundaries of the classroom is important to the continual development of teacher leaders.

Teachers take an interest in leadership roles when they realize their potential to inspire change in their schools and districts. In this regard, the promotion of their professional interests works as a gateway to engage them in broader leadership roles (Riveros et al., 2013). Within a culture that promotes building leadership capacity in a school, teacher leaders can continually evolve and serve as effective associated teacher educators.

REFERENCES

Allen, C., & Penuel, W. (2015). Studying teachers' sensemaking to investigate teachers' responses to professional development focused on new standards. *Journal of Teacher Education, 66*(2), 136–149. doi:0022487114560646

Association of Teacher Educators. (2008). *Standards for teacher educators*. Fairfax, VA: Author. Retrieved from http://www.ate1.org/pubs/uploads/tchredstds0308.pdf

Bacharach, N., Heck, T.W., & Dahlberg, K. (2010). Changing the face of student teaching through coteaching. *Action in Teacher Education, 32*(1), 3–14.

Barth, R.S. (2001). Teacher leader. *Phi Delta Kappan, 82*(6), 443–449.

Buffman, A., Mattos, M., & Weber, C. (2009). *Pyramid response to intervention: RTI, professional learning communities, and how to respond when kids don't learn*. Bloomington, IN: Solution Tree.

Carver, C., & Meier, J. (2013). Gaining confidence, managing conflict: Early career conceptions of teacher leadership during graduate coursework. *The New Educator, 9*(3), 173–191. doi:10.1080/1547688X.2013.806723

Collins, J. C. (2001). *Good to great: Why some companies make the leap—and others don't*. New York, NY: Harper Business.

Cook, L., & Friend, M. (1995). Co-teaching: Guidelines for creating effective practices. *Focus on Exceptional Children, 28*(3), 1–17.

Danielson, C. (2008). *The handbook for enhancing professional practice: Using the framework for teaching in your school*. Alexandria, VA: Association for Supervision and Curriculum Development.

DuFour, R., DuFour, R., Eaker, R., & Karhanek, G. (2004). *Whatever it takes: How professional learning communities respond when kids don't learn*. Bloomington, IN: The Solution Tree.

Ferriter, N., & Provenzano, N. (2013). Today's lesson: Self-directed learning . . . for teachers. *Phi Delta Kappan, 95*(3), 16–21. doi:10.1177/003172171309500305

Goodwin, C. (1994). Professional vision. *American Anthropologist, 96*(3), 606–633.

Gordon, J., & Smith, M. (2015). *You win in the locker room first: The 7 C's to building a winning team in business, sports, and life.* Hoboken, NJ: John Wiley & Sons.

Kazemi, E., & Hubbard, A. (2008). New directions for the design and study of professional development: Attending to the coevolution of teachers' participation across contexts. *Journal of Teacher Education, 59,* 428–441. doi:10.1177/0022487108324330

Kentucky Department of Education. (2015). *Leadership networks—Deliverables: Capacity building vs. train the trainer.* Retrieved from http://education.ky.gov/school/Pages/Leadership-Networks—-Deliverables.aspx

Kentucky Teacher Leadership Work Team. (2015). *Kentucky Teacher Leadership Framework.* Retrieved from http://education.ky.gov/teachers/Documents/Kentucky%20Teacher%20Leadership%20Framework.pdf

Lambert, L. (2003). *Leadership capacity for lasting school improvement.* Alexandria, VA: Association for Supervision and Curriculum Development.

Mangin, M., & Stoelinga, S. (2009). The future of instructional teacher leader roles. *The Educational Forum, 74*(1), 49–62. doi:10.1080/00131720903389208

Margolis, J., & Huggins, K. (2012). Distributed but undefined: New teacher leader roles to change schools. *Journal of School Leadership, 22*(5), 935–981.

Riveros, A., Netwon, P., & da Costa, J. (2013). From teachers to teacher-leaders: A case study. *International Journal of Teacher Leadership, 4*(1), 1–11. doi:10.1002/1098–2736(200102)38:2<137::AID-TEA1001>3.0.CO;2-U

vanDriel, J.H. (2001). Professional development and reform in science education: The role of teachers' practical knowledge. *Journal of Research in Science Teaching, 38*(2), 137–158.

Chapter Three

As the Moments Unfold

Developing Dispositions in Student Teacher–Mentor Teacher Relationships

Janine S. Davis and Victoria B. Fantozzi

ABSTRACT

This chapter draws on recent research on seven student teachers' interactions with their classroom teacher partners, direct perspectives and reflections of classroom teachers who have served in a mentoring role, and a theoretical framework that views interactions as stemming from dispositions that form within a community of practice, as well as within a system of persona creation and identity development. This chapter looked at the other side of the equation: the mentor teachers. Perspectives of the classroom teachers as viewed and recalled by the student teachers combine here with perspectives of mentor teachers to offer a more complete picture of what occurs during the complex interactions over a semester of student teaching. Implications for teacher education based on these mentor and student teacher perspectives are offered, to include reconsidering the evaluative role of mentors so that more genuine relationships may develop.

KEYWORDS

cooperating teachers, dispositions, identity, mentoring, mentor teachers, persona, student teachers, teacher educators

One of the most complicated aspects of mentoring student teachers is that there is no real consensus in the research about what a mentor teacher is or does (Ambrosetti & Dekker, 2010; Hamman & Romano, 2009; Hobson, 2010; Long et al., 2012; Maynard, 2000; Smith & Avetisan, 2011; Zeichner, 2005). Additionally, it is not common for schools of education to have systematic training for mentor teachers in the act of mentoring (Feiman-Nemser, 1998; Zeichner, 2002), and school practicum and internship sites can feel opposed to teacher education programs (Smagorinsky, Rhym, & Moore, 2013).

There are various calls in the literature to investigate aspects of successful mentoring in student teaching, such as the continuum of mentor roles (Kensington-Miller, 2005), which is explored further in Clarke, Triggs, and Nielsen (2014), and built on the commonly accepted roles of classroom placeholder (almost no involvement), supervisor of practica (mainly oversight), and teacher educator (a coach-like role, informed by current research).

As Flores and Day (2005) noted, these kinds of interactions during preservice training matter to future teaching identities. Those familiar with the work of mentors and student teachers may recognize the call of practice that these parties hear; student teachers and mentor teachers think: "This is where students are educated. Theory has its place, but this is the practice. This is reality."

In this chapter we offer a practical yet research-based take on the voices of student teachers and mentor teachers as they considered and negotiated the complexities of an often ill-defined but vitally important role and relationship.

PARTICIPANTS AND METHODS

The following findings drew on research on seven secondary-level student teachers' interactions with their classroom teacher partners during the student teaching semester and direct perspectives and reflections of classroom teachers who have served in a mentoring role. The purpose of this study was to determine the kinds of interactions between student teachers and mentor teachers (MTs), and how those MTs displayed various dispositions for mentoring within those interactions.

The student teacher participants were between the ages of 21 and 25 and were completing their initial teacher licensure at a large, competitive university in the Mid Atlantic. All names are pseudonyms. Methods for the primary study involved extensive interviews and analysis methods according to Lincoln and Guba (1985). The initial round of interviews did not include the perspectives of mentor teachers, only those of student teachers. For this study the findings from the initial phase were shared with mentor teachers during interviews exploring the mentor teachers' perspectives on student teaching.

As part of the theoretical framework for this study, we viewed interactions as stemming from dispositions that form within a community of practice (Lave & Wenger, 1991), as well as within a system of persona creation and identity development. Butler and Cuenca (2012) asserted that mentor teachers play one of three roles: mentor as emotional support, mentor as instructional coach, or mentor as socializing agent; the authors offer a fourth role, that of (for better or worse) the gatekeeper (Davis & Fantozzi, 2016).

The gatekeeper role, along with 10 others, has also been outlined in the recent review of the literature by Clarke, Triggs, and Nielsen (2014). Negotiating such roles while also maintaining a positive disposition for teaching and mentoring can be challenging, but there are strategies that can support the mentoring relationship when the classroom teacher is viewed as a teacher educator.

Building on dramaturgical theory, we positioned student teachers' and MTs' persona formation and actions as roles played based on expectations they hold of their perceived roles and relationships in the student teaching experience. We used the term *perceived roles* because the expectations for the roles of the MT and of the student teacher are not often explicitly discussed. Indeed, among our participants, none of the student teachers described having an explicit discussion with their MTs about expectations for each of their respective roles during the student teaching semester.

FINDINGS AND DISCUSSION

In order to best convey the structure of mentoring interactions as they unfolded during the semester, the following section combines both findings and discussion and organizes findings based on the timing of various phases during student teaching.

Before Student Teaching Begins

After a match was made between student teacher and mentor teacher (in this case, by the centralized university office for practicum placements in the education program), the two made contact before the student began to teach the class. The following were areas that emerged as useful considerations or, more notably, gaps in conversations for the student-mentor pairs as the MT negotiated his or her role (and often the students' university supervisors were present or involved in these early discussions).

The classroom context. Beyond discussion of what to expect in terms of the secondary students' levels of performance and perceived motivation, it was rare that mentors discussed the community in which the school was situated and the ways that their classroom related to the school as a whole. Similarly, the role of the classroom teacher's philosophy and when, why, or if it might change was not a focus of early discussions, but in one case this kind of conversation directly affected a student teacher's thinking.

Maria described shifting her interactions with students to be more casual and friendly in one class because her MT shared that that goals of the class (an elective) were more about increasing positive interaction than about evaluating students. Jan Mueller, an MT in a different setting, noted that a teaching philosophy was often not easily encapsulated in a brief meeting, but rather that it emerged through a series of interactions with students, parents, and teaching colleagues.

She believed that showing what kinds of teaching she valued for her students (in her case, cooperative learning, projects, and discussions) over time demonstrated her philosophy better than a statement might.

Honing observational skills. During early interactions the student teachers described assessing the verbal messages of their MTs, who gave advice on aspects to expect such as patterns of student behavior, grading practices, school policies, and upcoming units. While the student teachers recalled these early conversations (many of them briefed or sent over e-mail), students also assessed nonverbal messages during face-to-face meetings and drew on their initial impressions of their mentors to project what the mentoring experience might be like. Maria had three MTs and noted,

> Working with the other two MTs . . . was a surprise, because I didn't know I would be working with other teachers. My main MT talked a lot about what their personalities were . . . I kind of like chose them, the other two people that I work with, based on observing and hanging out with them the first week of school, so my personality meshed well, just being with them, but it was, you know, as the semester went on, it was different than what I thought, you know, initial first impressions.

Still other student teachers had expectations of how often their MTs would be present, or how involved they would be during lessons, but in every case these were not explicitly stated in early meetings. In one case, Katelyn was distraught when her MT who was present often early in the placement, started leaving the classroom on a regular basis.

In response to these findings, Ms. Mueller notes that she would plan to have such conversations from the beginning of the experience if she has another student teacher. However, she added that over the semester, her particular student teacher showed signs of being ready to teach independently, and so she left the room more often. In some cases that she had observed, the MT had sensed that the student teacher needed the support from an MT in the room more often.

Taken together, these perspectives suggest an occasional disconnect between the MT and student teacher in when and how often the MT would leave the room. While student teachers generally preferred to be alone, there was a fine balance, and Katelyn felt abandoned, while Maria felt stifled. Clark was happy to be left alone, while Tina wanted her MT to be present and interacting with students in the classroom often. Maintaining a disposition of trust, responsiveness, and willingness to let the class unfold without MT supervision was something that most of the student teachers wished of their MTs, but did not request, and when MTs met their student teacher's level of preference, they appeared to do this subconsciously, without prior negotiation and as the moments unfolded.

The role of research and inquiry. This teacher education program had capstone research projects that students began to plan during student teaching in the fall. While none of the mentors or student teachers described this as a key part of their interactions or dispositions, some of the more involved mentors shared informal methods that they had used to approach planning and teaching their courses, which had the effect of influencing student teachers' actions and thinking.

Tina described a time when her MT had advised her to offer fewer stations to the general earth science class as compared to the advanced class because she had found it to be more manageable in the past. Clark described learning about the research support for the scripted program he taught in some of his courses from his MT—the MT had conveyed a respect for research in their interactions, which had then become a part of Clark's considerations about teaching.

A scholarly disposition for MTs was common to this school district context, where the university was a major force and common alma mater for many teachers and all of the student teachers in the district schools (even ones not involved in this study). It was not uncommon for teachers to openly question administrative policies if they believed they lacked research support. These findings, particularly that the student teachers entered into the experience with certain expectations that can lead to tension if they are not met (such as hoping for guidance, but being left alone), echoed previous studies such as Hamman and Romano (2009), who noted that these early expectations can contribute to role confusion for MTs (p. 7).

The Early Days

Interactions during the early days and weeks of student teaching shaped later successes and challenges. When conversations centered around setting goals for interaction, student teachers felt more comfortable and confident during their lessons.

Setting goals for teaching. The content, lessons, and units that the student teacher would teach were often the primary focus of initial discussions because many saw it as a concrete topic for discussion. One major exception was Katelyn, who said "I have never talked to my MT about a lesson plan, I've never talked to her about anything. . . . I totally do my own thing being that she is gone 99.9% of the time." This was a highly unusual situation among the participants; in fact, many student teacher-mentor pairs had lesson plans that gradually reverted to the MT taking charge of the lesson or fighting herself to avoid doing so. Tina felt freedom to innovate within boundaries; she said,

> I try to stick to the schedule as far as what she thinks we should be teaching each day, so I've never tried to go off of that, but as far as like activities that I do each day, like I feel totally comfortable, I feel like I have the freedom to change things up a bit whenever I want to . . . she'll suggest things but she doesn't demand that I do certain things. Like we do have this quarter-long scrapbook project that we're having them do; she really wanted to do it, it's the first year, but as far as daily activities and stuff, she might be like, "oh this worked really well," and then so I'll want to use it, but she never mandates that I do something in particular.

Kara added that lesson planning was linked to her view of who was the main teacher in the classroom. She noted,

> There was a day or two where she (her MT) wasn't there and she was like, "oh, will you teach my lessons," and I was teaching her lesson and doing what she planned and stuff and it was kind of like, I guess I am not "the teacher." I think for me it was I planned out the lesson I planned it all and that is what makes me the head teacher.

Both Kara and Jamie agreed that it was when they were planning their own lessons that they felt like the head teacher.

Setting goals for interaction. Our research showed that when conversations focused on the kind and level of interactions that would unfold during the semester, the student teachers and MTs felt more confident in their roles, with one notable exception. These kinds of interactions included colleagues such as other members of professional learning communities (PLCs) or neighboring teachers. In one extreme example, Katelyn actually found support from a neighboring student teacher instead of the assigned MT because her MT was often away from the room. Jamie also negotiated interactions with a neighboring teacher, saying,

> I feel like, my MT is pretty good about if I have an idea, she is like "Go for it!" but for me the whole team planning is interesting because, um . . . Aaron [a neighboring teacher] and my MT have taught together for like four years, so

they have four years of material that they used together, so he gets very uncomfortable about stepping away from that.

Maria knew her MT from earlier years, so the two discussed their relationship and Maria felt that she was mentally prepared for what was to come. She said,

> I knew, going into this semester . . . that it would be challenging, like forming a professional relationship, versus having her as a teacher, she's older, and a more seasoned teacher, so she's very motherly and maternal to her students and I'm her former student, now a colleague. So I kind of knew coming in that she was going to be someone that I would have to figure out, as far as what our relationship would be like. . . . And I guess because I had her in high school, she's like a firecracker type person, tell you like it is, so I was like, okay, gotta not take things personal, so I kind of mentally prepared for those aspects, and prepared for . . . the communication that needs to happen; you have to be the teacher in the class. When they interrupt, I didn't expect that part to be such a challenge.

An exception to the link between planned interactions and confidence was Clark. He displayed and felt very confident, but casual—he constructed this persona intentionally—but wanted to be free to work out his own approach to teaching without what he saw as interference from the MT. Clark said,

> I think if there's that constant stopping from an outside force, it's not natural. It doesn't train a student—teacher—to think on their feet, to really deal with the person, to deal with it their own way. Because the student teacher might have a way that really works, but the MT might not prefer it or the MT hasn't tried it, but it really works for the individual, and people have to make mistakes on their own and they have to learn on their own, they can only develop a style that works specifically for them.

He had not stated this desire to be left alone, but his MT was comfortable with working in or out of the room without interrupting, even when Clark made errors in his instruction (his MT would bring these up in later casual meetings.) Clark's desire to "make mistakes and learn on his own" was unique; the others wanted their teachers to leave the classroom occasionally, but none of them wanted or expected to make mistakes during that unsupervised time.

What was similar to some of the others is that Clark did not state these wishes to his MT: they simply developed over time and were unstated.

Negotiating the line between independence, planning, and support. Some of the most complicated conversations (or missing conversations) centered on how to negotiate control in the classroom in terms of classroom management, including who would determine and enforce the rules. Jessica noted, "My MT [said], 'I don't you care if you change the way the class is structured, but there are certain things I want to enforce because I need to take back over and they need to be following my rules.'"

Jessica's approach to students might have differed from her MT's, but this explicit conversation helped Jessica to work within her MT's system. Kara had mixed feelings about her MT's approach to the students because they had different approaches to relationships with the students. She said,

> She is a little more . . . not strict, but a little more intense about stuff that the students are doing than I am. So it's kind of hard for me, just homework assignments and she will be like, "grade it on this and this and this." And I am like, "it's homework!" I wouldn't do it as intense as that, but I kind of have to because it's her class. . . . And when she is not there I can just do my own thing, and I like to have chances to kind of just like chat with the students, and she does less of the whole like chat with the kids and try to get to know them.

Rather than discuss the differences in their approaches to student relationships with her MT, Kara chose to stick to the policies that her MT had laid out, and try out her way with students when her MT was out of the room. Katelyn felt that the dynamic changed when her MT entered the room, because both the students and Katelyn felt that the MT had more power. She noted, "There is a certain amount of power I will never have because I am a student teacher . . . when my MT walks in the room, it's just a different feeling, like I think they expect her to call them out, but when I call them out, it's like, 'Can I get away with ignoring her?' . . . I am not a threat."

Kara found that she learned from the students' preferences as well as her MT's. Kara noted,

> What my MT had them do was just very straightforward have them take notes, so I was like, "ok I guess that's how they learn best; that is what they want," but now that I know them better and I get to talk to them and I have had some time one-on-one where we can hang out with them and I am like—"what do you guys actually want to do?" And they tell me what they would like to do and how it could be more engaging and stuff for them.

Some indicated wanting less mentor involvement, while others wanted more feedback. Knowing when and how often to leave the room was a delicate balance, but Jessica felt as if her MT achieved that balance. She noted,

> I've kind of had the best of both worlds here where my MT will disappear for a while, but we talk about what happened and I will mention certain things. She'll be there for my really bad class, or she will offer her suggestions as much as she can offer on this class. But lots of times she will be like "Ok, I'm going to go be in so and so's class for next block."

In addition to working out when the MT would be present, so too did some pairs determine how they would interact in front of the students (an added dimension that complicated the relationship and the available dispositions for the MT, who in many cases was also attempting to fade into the background so that the students would view the student teacher as an authority figure).

Establishing patterns of mentorship and modeling. Some pairs developed creative solutions to mentoring with an audience of students also in the room. One mentor-student teacher pair established a signal whereby the student teacher would wave, and the mentor would retreat from the teaching role, and the student teacher would assume responsibility for the lesson. Maria said,

> Doctora and I sat down and I said, "I have that kind of personality where if you interject and start saying something, I will just by nature sort of back off. I won't like try to come back in, I don't know how to transition back, I will just back off and let you finish your thought and keep going," because that's kind of what she did a few times in the beginning, and that's what [my other MT] did in the last few weeks, so we started this system where we pass off. And we both acknowledged that she talked a lot, and after a period when I was head teacher and she started seeing my style, she started just leaving then so that I could have class, and I think that's something, with my other MTs we got to a point where we were just tackling classroom issues, like behavior management stuff that's going on.

Maria's MT was familiar with mentoring because she had had several student teachers in past years, but Maria appreciated that she never dictated the kind of teacher she thought Maria should be. This outward identification of dispositions was unique, though; Maria accepted how she was likely to react and anticipated how the MT would react, and they developed a solution based on these patterns of interaction.

Jamie found that she had to ask for help when she wanted it, but that the absence was not negative, saying, "My MT, she peaces out a lot, but if I have questions she is always is willing to look over my stuff so just having an extra pair of eyes to re-assure myself that it is correct or it's a good way to do it . . . I feel like if I need support I can ask her." Katelyn found that although her mentor was not present in the room, she could talk over classroom management issues with her, and said,

> Yeah, my MT because she was absent [working on a grant] she offered me a lot of behavior management support, which I definitely needed, so I am thankful for her—we would debrief I would tell her how classes went and what the problems were, and she would like help me figure out, "okay, what can you do?"

In response, Ms. Mueller noted,

> It is so hard to read them [the student teachers] sometimes, because they are so stressed and they want to do well and help the students, but they also need to

improve in lots of ways. I just think it worked best to give them small doses of input based on what they [the student teachers] notice is going on. . . . I try to steer them towards the things they really need to work on.

This sense of parceling out input appeared in multiple recollections from the student teachers; some seemed to crave constant feedback, but they felt as if their mentors were waiting until they felt the time was right, there was time to address it, or they sensed the student teacher was able or ready to hear it.

Finding a Routine and Relationships

Daily interactions. Many (but not all) mentors developed a process for checking in informally with their student teachers and utilizing what appeared to be subconscious modeling of how to interact with students and colleagues. The student teachers indicated that they watched these interactions and incorporated these behaviors into their own interactions. Tina said, "I forced myself to be more confident . . . I kind of used Betty as a model for that."

Maria also noted,

> I became more student-sensitive than I thought I would . . . I guess that's a little bit of Catrina's influence on me. She's a very student-sensitive . . . from the beginning I was very much aware of how my primary MT, Doctora, was doing things and I was thinking I needed to come in as authoritarian, my way or the highway, and I think there needs to be decisions that are made purely by the teacher, but I see the teacher sensitivity to student needs radar has gone up a little bit.

In these ways the student teachers observed their MTs' dispositions as teachers, but their dispositions as mentors were another aspect of which the student teachers became aware.

Determining how and when the student teacher would take charge was a common theme that arose for all of the participants, although Katelyn noted that "I am not even sure if she knows what I did today so . . . not in a bad [way], not because she doesn't care," adding later that she took this to mean that her MT trusted her to make daily instructional decisions without always being present in the room to observe them. Maria said,

> I feel like I didn't have enough time in the beginning to see Doctora do things to kind of be comfortable, you just kind of jump in after a couple of weeks. And I'd be like how do I teach this? And she would be like, "no, you decide, I'm hands off" . . . and she'd say, "I don't want you to do exactly what I do, so, I think that was kind of a weakness for me." I think I got better at it, getting in front and explaining things and I had to do it a lot, so the more I had to do it I got better at it.

Furthermore, Clark noted that his MT also worked to help him feel confident by retreating during class sessions and checking in briefly about how the day had gone, saying,

> Mr. Brock was helpful, we have to keep things moving. Just speaking with him and looking at what you planned and covered that day gives you an idea of how to pace things . . . it's his classroom, but I kind of trust . . . it's his subject, it's what he's been doing, and I really pay attention because he has a say. It's his classroom and he doesn't want to have like a giant hole to fix in the boat when he gets back, and part of that is being considerate to him. So I would say he was a big influence, I'm trying to give him what he needs, what he wants, and at the same time, with the students, what they need and what they want.

Clark's comment that he was trying to "give him what he needs" gets at an issue that lurked under the surface for all of the student teachers, but was never mentioned aloud around their MTs. This issue was that the student teachers knew that the MTs would recommend them for future jobs, and so they wanted to keep them happy and disguise any displeasure. More on this power imbalance appears in a later section on the evaluative role of mentors.

Casual meetings. Casual teaching observations were much less stressful for the student teachers as compared to their observations from university supervisors, since those occurred much less often and in most cases, the students had to submit a lesson plan in advance of the observation. Many breakthroughs occurred during casual meetings like the ones noted earlier, when student teachers would check in about certain students or about their personal progress with their MT. The MTs also developed their dispositions during meetings like these, in much the same way that a friendship might develop over time.

Clark found his MT to be "very professional, but flexible at the same time. He doesn't ask a lot of questions. All he wants me to do is give him the game plan . . . and if he has an objection, which he rarely does, he'll usually offer me feedback and it's never negative."

Clark's casual meetings and interactions with his MT were similar to others, including Tina, who said, "She's been very accepting and open and willing to use different ideas and take into consideration other ideas . . . she never mandates that I do something in particular." Maria described her MT as "motherly and maternal" to her students, but that they worked to find a professional relationship with each other.

Modeling teaching, reflection, triumph, and struggle. How did mentors show how they negotiated internal and external conflict around teaching, reflection, triumph, and struggle? Student teachers recalled when their MT responded positively to their work by actually using the student teacher–planned lessons in other courses. Jessica's MT said, "I really did like this [method of teaching] and I want to use that in the future." It was through such interactions that some student teachers came to appreciate an open-minded, flexible disposition from their MTs, as evidenced by a willingness to use materials created by someone with less experience.

Maria's main MT, who had had several student teachers, told her, "It's hard for me to lose control." This meant that she wanted to allow Maria the freedom and independence to be the main teacher in the classroom, but that she struggled with a change in her own role in relation to the students. Furthermore, Maria's second MT struggled visibly with knowing when to interject about content or classroom management.

After years spent honing her own confident persona in relation to the students, Maria's second MT—this was her first student teacher—was having the opposite experience of feeling as if she had to fade into the background and become less involved, less of a leader in the classroom.

At a time when reading the situation and Maria's response would have been ideal (and for an MT who was proud to be sensitive to students' needs and conflict-free pedagogy), she did not feel comfortable stepping back and allowing Maria to lead. This MT vulnerability recalls Maynard (2000), and indeed, the participants did describe a kind of management of their MTs.

Late in the Game

As the experience came to an end, student teachers had to extricate themselves from the classroom as well as from the relationship with their MT. At times this meant addressing (or, in some cases, ignoring) issues that arose in the relationship, dealing with evaluations, and reflecting on the experience.

Troubleshooting when things go wrong. Flexibility and humility were especially crucial for all parties involved in the student teaching experience, from the mentor to the supervisor to the student teacher and even colleagues or PLC members. The MTs in this study seemed generally unaware of their student teachers' discontent when it existed. In several situations this lack of knowledge was purposeful on the part of the student teachers, who did not want to confront their MTs about any dissatisfaction because of the role that MTs played in evaluating and recommending student teachers for future jobs.

Katelyn said,

> I mean I feel like they made it sound like if you don't get a good recommendation from your MT then it's going to be really hard to find a job and it's going to be very unfavorable; honestly if the recommendation was not hanging over my head, I think I would have been more vocal.

This was in keeping with recent findings that the MT can play a kind of gatekeeper role (Clarke et al., 2014; Davis & Fantozzi, 2016).

The evaluative role. Perhaps one of the most challenging aspects of forming a true mentor relationship with a student teacher was the evaluative role that mentors served. Some form of the statement "She will be writing my recommendation someday" appeared in at least five interviews with student teachers; Katelyn described it as "hanging over her head." Ms. Mueller recalled that this was one aspect of mentoring that felt uncomfortable; she said, "I felt as if he never really admitted when things were going badly, and that there was a kind of unspoken agreement that he would not be too needy as long as I would be helpful for him when it came time to find a job."

Those familiar with the show *Project Runway* or even most new teacher induction programs will recognize that in many other mentoring partnerships, the evaluation is done by outside parties to avoid tainting the relationship. The role of evaluator affected an MT's dispositions because, much as a mandated reporter cannot promise total secrecy and confidentiality, so too must a mentor temper a caring and open persona with the seriousness and professionalism that an evaluator must take on. When mentor teachers evaluate student teachers, it can affect the student teachers' identity development (Grossman, Smagorinsky, & Valencia, 1999; Valencia, Martin, Place, & Grossman, 2009), and there are issues of power imbalance in student teaching (Anderson, 2007; Rippon & Martin, 2003) at play in this situation as well.

Formal meetings. In addition to formal teaching observations as scheduled in advance and which often also involved the university supervisor, this teacher education program requested that mentor teachers meet regularly (such as once a week during planning time) with their student teachers to offer advice and feedback on their progress. Some pairs observed these meeting times more frequently than others.

For some student teachers the observation is seen not as an opportunity to learn, but as an evaluation of their teaching; the observation marks their teaching as either good or bad, rather than that the observation will give them feedback on strengths and weaknesses. (See Fantozzi, 2013.) Even without the formal meetings many of the student teachers are acutely aware of the evaluative role of the MT. Kara said, "I feel like when she is there, there is always kind of in the back of my mind—don't mess up, don't mess up—that kind of thing."

Reflecting on the experience. It is said so often when supporting student teachers after they teach lessons independently that it's almost a cliche: "what worked and what didn't?" By the time the end of the semester came, the student teachers described being able to see the highs and lows of the experience, and nearly all were thankful for the times (whether requested or not) that MTs encouraged them to consider what was working and what was not.

Some messages from MTs that the student teachers recalled were global recommendations about disposition and time management. One MT displayed an embroidered sign reading, "say no to the committee meetings." Katelyn recalled,

> I talked to my MT because she has been teaching for 20 years and I was like, "what do you contribute your longevity to?" And she is like, "I leave at 4:00 every day." And I thought that is really good because we think, "Oh, I worked so hard in college, this will just automatically transfer into these long hours teaching," but I feel like you need to be smarter with your time rather than just spend hours upon hours at school, because . . . she said, "You could stay here forever, there is always something else you could be doing, there is always something that you could be tweaking, but just say nope. This is how I am setting a boundary for myself."

MTs reflected as well, although their timing was less rigid than the student teachers, who hoped to begin a full-time teaching job in just a few months. The MTs did not know if and when they might have another student teacher. In addition, there was no set opportunity for MTs to reflect on their experiences or their performance. Final meetings were focused on student teacher growth and reflection.

The ways that MTs might have grown, the MT's dispositions, style of feedback, role as a supporter or co-teacher, or even "what worked and what didn't" were not topics for discussion. This may be an interesting area for new study: How might the opportunity to reflect help mentor teachers become better mentors? This is not to suggest that the student teachers' reflection is not paramount, but that this would be an additional part of the relationship between the university and the mentor teacher and the role of the mentor teacher.

Implications and Recommendations

Given the perspectives of the student teachers and MTs in this study around how MTs developed and displayed dispositions for mentoring, we offer some recommendations for the student teaching experience.

First, an awareness of the kinds of dispositions that MTs can and do develop should figure into more discussions in teacher education coursework and during the mentoring experience. Furthermore, effective ways of responding to challenges and struggles (such as explicit meetings about how and when the student teacher will be alone in the classroom, and why) would be a logical addition to a list of regular conversations that should take place between the student teacher and MT.

Second, the evaluative role that MTs serve in most teacher education programs affects the kind of relationship that develops, and should be reconsidered. More integrated teacher education faculty and supervisors who incorporate feedback from MTs into their evaluations may enable student teachers and MTs to develop more genuine and honest interactions, because student teachers may not have to mask their frustrations if the experience is negative in various ways.

Third, this study begins to uncover dispositions of MTs that have various effects on student teachers, but there is more work to be done in the form of larger-scale research that might codify some of these findings and, ultimately, translate them into methods of matching student teachers and MTs more effectively.

One limitation of this study was that we gleaned MT perspectives indirectly in most cases (e.g., a student teacher's recollection of what a mentor said, or the thoughts of an MT not directly involved in the setting). Future research should include these MT perspectives as they develop before, during, and after the student teaching experience.

It is possible that one reason these perspectives were limited in the research is that teacher educators recognize the hours of time that MTs already commit to their student teachers, and do not wish to burden them further by asking them to complete additional research requirements. MTs also may be interested researchers themselves who have overwhelming demands on their time.

However, learning more from this vital member of the overall process of educating new teachers is a gap that we must fill if we are to understand how interactions and dispositions for both teaching and for mentoring develop. How and where do successful MTs learn to mentor well? Does it depend on their student teachers, and, if so, what makes for an ideal match? These are questions that future research must continue to investigate.

CONCLUSION

Mentor teachers can have a strong influence on their student teachers' teaching practices and interactions (Rozelle & Wilson, 2012), and the findings from this study support this claim. The relationship between MTs, university-based teacher educators and supervisors, and student teachers is an intricate web of intra- and interpersonal development, to include learning from research, one's practice, colleagues, students, the context, and each other. It is a rare web indeed where all members are equal partners in this exchange and emerge with a feeling of success and confidence.

This chapter aims to share the voices of student teachers and MTs as they recall their challenges and triumphs so that we may learn from their experiences and offer considerations for future partners in the student teaching experience, especially the MT. Learning within a community of practice (Lave & Wenger, 1991) means that all members of the community grow and change and develop skills both during and as a result of the experience; this is not the same as learning theory and then applying it (Davies, 2005). There are at least two ways that mentors and student teachers might miss out on the benefits of being partners in a true community of practice.

First, if the aim is for one party (in this case, the student teacher) to learn teaching skills from the other party (the MT) in a one-way interaction in order to implement those teaching skills in the future, then the pupils and student teacher miss out on the chance to benefit from increasing skills and knowledge as student teaching unfolds, and the MT loses the chance to develop skills as a mentor and as a teacher.

Also, if student teachers view their MT as a kind of gatekeeper (or the MT views himself or herself as such), then the entire community will lose the chance for transformational growth and change. Dispositions can be a complex and even controversial business; they necessitate careful definition for teachers when used for evaluation (Damon, 2007), and the same is true for mentor teachers.

REFERENCES

Ambrosetti, A., & Dekker, J. (2010). The interconnectedness of roles of mentors and mentees in pre-service teacher education mentoring relationships. *Australian Journal of Teacher Education, 35*(6), 42–55.

Anderson, D. (2007). The role of cooperating teachers' power in student teaching. *Education, 128*, 307–323.

Butler, B., & Cuenca, A. (2012). Conceptualizing the roles of mentor teachers during student teaching. *Action in Teacher Education, 34*(4), 296–308. doi: 10.1080/01626620.2012.717012

Clarke, A., Triggs, V., & Nielsen, W. (2014). Cooperating teacher participation in teacher education: A review of the literature. *Review of Educational Research, 84*(2), 163–202.

Damon, W. (2007). Dispositions and teacher assessment: The need for a more rigorous definition. *Journal of Teacher Education, 58*(5), 365–369.

Davies, B. (2005). Communities of practice: Legitimacy not choice. *Journal of Sociolinguistics, 9*(4), 557–581.

Davis, J.S. & Fantozzi, V.B. (2016). What do student teachers want in mentor teachers? Desired, expected, possible, and emerging roles. *Mentoring and Tutoring, 24*(3), 250–266. doi: http://dx.doi.org/10.1080/13611267.2016.1222814

Fantozzi, V.B. (2013). "Oh god, she is looking at every little thing I am doing!" Student teachers' constructions of the observation experience. *Current Issues in Education, 16*(1), 1–12.

Feiman-Nemser, S. (1998). Teachers as teacher educators. *European Journal of Teacher Education, 21*(1), 63–74.

Flores, M.A., & Day, C. (2005). Contexts which shape and reshape new teachers' identities: A multi-perspective study. *Teaching and Teacher Education, 22*(2), 219–232.

Grossman, P., Smagorinsky, P., & Valencia, S. (1999). Appropriating tools for teaching English: A theoretical framework for research on learning to teach. *American Journal of Education, 108*(1), 1–29.

Hamman, D., & Romano, J.E. (2009). The desired cooperator: Preservice preferences and role confusion during the teaching practicum. *Current Issues in Education, 11*(4). Retrieved from http://cie.asu.edu/ojs/index.php/cieatasu/article/viewFile/1576/620

Hobson, A. (2010). On being on the bottom of the pecking order: Beginner teachers' perceptions and experiences of support. *Teacher Development, 13*(4), 299–320.

Kensington-Miller, B. (2005). Mentoring mathematics teachers in low socio-economic secondary schools in New Zealand. *The New Zealand Mathematics Magazine, 42*(2), 1–12.

Lave, J., & Wenger, E. (1991). *Situated learning: Legitimate peripheral participation.* Cambridge: Cambridge University Press.

Lincoln, Y.S., & Guba, E.G. (1985). *Naturalistic inquiry.* Beverly Hills, CA: Sage.

Long, J.S., McKenzie-Robblee, S., Schaefer, L., Steeves, P., Wnuk, S., Pinnegar, E., & Clandinin, D.J. (2012). Literature review on induction and mentoring related to early career teacher attrition and retention. *Mentoring and Tutoring: Partnership in Learning 20*(6), 7–26. doi: 10.1080/13611267.2012.645599

Maynard, T. (2000). Learning to teach or learning to manage mentors? Experiences of school based teacher training. *Mentoring and Tutoring, 8*(1), 17–30. doi: 10.1080/713685510

Rippon, J., & Martin, M. (2003) Supporting induction: Relationships count. *Mentoring and Tutoring, 11*(2), 211–226.

Rozelle, J.J., & Wilson, S.M. (2012). Opening the black box of field experiences: How cooperating teachers' beliefs and practices shape student teachers' beliefs and practices. *Teaching and Teacher Education, 28*(8), 1196–1205.

Smagorinsky, P., Rhym, D., & Moore, C.P. (2013). Competing centers of gravity: A beginning English teacher's socialization process within conflictual settings. *English Education, 45*(2), 147.

Smith, E., & Avetisan, V. (2011). Learning to teach with two mentors: Revisiting the "two worlds pitfall" in student teaching. *The Teacher Educator, 46,* 335–354. doi: 10.1080/08878730.2011.604400

Valencia, S., Martin, S., Place, N., & Grossman, P. (2009). Complex interactions in student teaching: Lost opportunities for learning. *Journal of Teacher Education, 60*(3), 304–322. doi: 10.1177/0022487109336543

Zeichner, K. (2002). Beyond traditional structures of student teaching. *Teacher Education Quarterly,* 59–64.

Zeichner, K.M. (2005). A research agenda for teacher education. In M. Cochran-Smith and K.M. Zeichner (Eds.), *Studying teacher education: The Report of the AERA Panel on Research and Teacher Education* (pp. 737–757). London: Routledge.

Chapter Four

An Enhanced Role for Classroom Teachers During Student Teaching

Effective Collaboration Within a Professional Learning Community

Billi L. Bromer

ABSTRACT

The development of a professional learning community during student teaching highlights the important role of classroom teachers as teacher educators during clinical placements. Because collaboration within a professional learning community requires participants to examine their own beliefs and personal practices, the process takes time and careful attention to the interpersonal aspects of effective communication. As educator preparation programs undergo review and scrutiny, the importance of effective collaboration between program providers and P-12 schools becomes vital. There is need for further research on the interpersonal factors that can assure effective collaboration within professional learning communities and how preparation for participation in a collaborative environment can be embedded within educator preparation. With this approach comes an enhanced and vital role for classroom teachers as associated teacher educators.

KEYWORDS

Collaboration, collaborative culture, interpersonal communication, preservice teachers, professional learning communities, teacher candidates

LAYING THE GROUNDWORK FOR COLLABORATION

Previous and more traditional approaches to teaching as individual and personal practice often produced new teacher feelings of being overwhelmed with responsibility and being isolated in the ability to address them (Feiman-Nemser, 1998, 2012; Lieberman & Miller, 2011). The National Commission on Teaching and America's Future (NCTAF) has reported that 14% of teachers leave the field after the first year and 46% leave after the fifth year (National Commission on Teaching and America's Future, 2003).

The report highlighted a serious dilemma in education and inspired future summits to address the problem. A subsequent report from the same commission urged the development of a 21st-century teaching model that focused on a more integrated professional culture rather than the solo teaching approach of traditional programs (NCTAF, 2005). Educator preparation programs of the past have not prepared teachers with a realistic vision of what is needed for today's students to learn (Chesley & Jordan, 2012), and university course work followed by several weeks of student teaching is no longer the recommended format, according to Darling-Hammond (as cited in Scherer, 2012).

Classroom teachers and teacher education program faculty are natural partners in educator preparation. With the advent of standards-based teaching and greater accountability for learner outcomes, university-school partnerships have become the hallmark of quality educator preparation programs.

In 2013 the Council of Chief State Officers' Interstate Teacher Assessment (InTASC) and, in 2015, the Council for the Accreditation of Educator Preparation (CAEP) each urged the development of improved collaboration among teacher candidates, the classroom teachers in whose rooms teacher candidates are placed for clinical work, and the university faculty who supervise teacher candidates during student teaching.

Within well-constructed higher education and P-12 school partnerships are opportunities to create the collaborative culture recommended by both CAEP and InTASC and to engage in the dialogues between experienced teaching professionals and teacher candidates, often reflective in nature, that can occur as an outcome (Bates, Ramirez, & Drits, 2009; Hoaglund, Birkenfield, & Box, 2014; Lawley, Moore, & Smajic, 2014).

MEETING THE STANDARDS OF CAEP AND INTASC

CAEP Standards

The newly developed CAEP standards address the components of effective teaching (Council for the Accreditation of Educator Preparation, 2015). The standards are a guide for educator preparation providers who wish to serve as strong models for quality teaching. The standards emerged from research indicators of what factors are most likely to impact outcomes for students.

Standard 2: Clinical Partnerships and Practice requires educator preparation program providers to "ensure that effective partnerships and high-quality practice are central to preparation so that candidates develop the knowledge, skills, and professional disposition necessary to demonstrate positive impact on all P-12 students' learning and development" (p. 6). Standard 2 consists of three areas of focus: (a) partnerships for clinical preparation, (b) clinical educators, and (c) clinical experiences.

The rationale for the importance of clinical partnerships between educator preparation programs and P-12 school districts or schools is the collaborative nature of the partnerships and a shared approach to improve student learning. CAEP characterized the partnerships based on acceptance of that goal among all stakeholders. Shared training is the natural outcome when strong P-12 school and university partnerships are created that permit university and P-12 school professionals to become colleagues in educator preparation. The shared training responsibility between university educators and the classroom teachers in the P-12 settings who guide and mentor preservice teachers makes vivid the ways in which classroom teachers serve as teacher educators in educator preparation programs (Bullough, Draper, Smith, & Birrell, 2004; Korth, Erickson, & Hall, 2009).

InTASC Standards

In April 2013 InTASC revised its 2011 Model Core Teaching Standards and provided a vision for 21st-century teaching (Council of Chief State School Officers, 2013). That vision included the development of an atmosphere of collaboration that encourages collegiality and embraces shared professional learning.

The 10 standards have continued to focus on the knowledge, skills, and dispositions that have traditionally been the foundation of educator preparation and are grouped into four general categories of (a) the learner and learning, (b) content, (c) instructional practice, and (d) professional responsibility.

To develop professional responsibility, candidates need opportunities to reflect on their own practice, both on their own and through a framework of collaboration with others. Standard 9, Professional Learning and Ethical Practice, promotes the availability of professional learning opportunities at the earliest stages of candidate preparation. The revised InTASC standards also included a general guide on how to move toward that vision. InTASC's Learning Progression for Teachers addresses and accompanies each standard (Council of Chief State Officers, 2013).

The Learning Progression continuum for Standard 9, Professional Learning and Ethical Practice, recommends that a teacher "engages in structured individual and group learning opportunities" and "actively seeks professional community" (p. 42) at the initial point in the progression.

Association of Teacher Educators Standards

Nine standards for teacher educators were developed by the Association of Teacher Educators (ATE) to provide specific indicators of effective teacher education (Association of Teacher Educators, n.d.a). The standards provide a framework for teacher educators to assess their own professional practice. The standards are consistent with the goals of both CAEP and InTASC regarding the need for a collaborative and reflective professional environment.

The indicators of Standard 1, Teaching, suggest that teacher educators show evidence of reflective practice. The indicators of Standard 4, Professional Development, suggest that teacher educators continuously reflect on their teaching.

ATE believes that teacher educators are defined as those who instruct teachers or conduct research regarding teaching, including those outside of higher education. The growing focus on higher education and P-12 school partnerships has provided an ongoing opportunity for teacher educators to practice these standards (ATE, n.d.b).

CAEP (2015) also recommended that clinical experiences provided within the partnered framework between universities and P-12 schools be opportunities for teacher candidates to reflect upon the elements of their emerging practice and highlighted the "wisdom of practice" (p. 8) as an outcome of such reflection.

CREATING A COLLABORATIVE ENVIRONMENT DURING CLINICAL EXPERIENCES

To provide opportunities for teacher candidates to learn to work within a collegial environment, teacher educators must practice and model collaboration. Framing educator preparation within the concept of a collaborative professional culture provides an enhanced role as a teacher educator for the cooperating teachers who serve as mentors to student teachers. Classroom teachers may be underutilized as a valuable resource in guiding student teachers toward the partnership skills needed for effective teaching.

Educators who are involved in team planning across the same grade level or interaction with colleagues across other grade levels have valuable insight into how to initiate and maintain joint efforts. They may also have experience in what strategies are effective when working with colleagues. It is time to rethink educator preparation to create opportunities for teacher candidates, in concert with their cooperating teacher and university supervisors, to learn and practice the collaborative skills needed by new teachers to attain student learning.

However, for classroom teachers more accustomed to teaching as a solo practice or university supervisors who have little experience teaching candidates how to engage in a team process, this may present a challenge (Lieberman & Miller, 2011).

CAEP (2015) has recognized that educator preparation providers and P-12 schools both employ educators who possess unique skills and experiences that together can provide future teachers with the knowledge, skills, and dispositions needed for effective teaching. Partnering in what CAEP has identified as a "collaborative partnership" (p. 7) can assure that teacher candidates have opportunities to not only learn but also view and be able to demonstrate effective pedagogy.

InTASC has described education as evolving into a system in which a "continuous self-improvement embraced by . . . collaboration" prevails (Council of Chief State School Officers, 2013, p. 9).

Teaching is no longer behind a closed classroom door all day with one teacher and many students. Teaching is more visible and open to others for observation and feedback on professional practices. It is shared with colleagues through the analysis of classroom data for the purpose of improving student learning. The National Commission on Teaching and America's Future (2005) has described teaching as occurring within a "community of practice" (p. 3) in which teachers at all levels of experience share the goal of improving professional practice.

It is possible and likely that novice teachers may possess unique talents that experienced educators may not have, such as expertise in technology or creativity in infusing the arts. In addition to learning from veteran teachers, in a partnered relationship teacher candidates may have opportunities to instruct or mentor.

As teacher candidates participate in clinical experiences at all stages of preparation, they are provided opportunities to experience the ongoing teamwork that is a key element of effective teaching and must be willing to participate in the learning communities in which such cooperation can be effectively developed.

To actively engage in a collaborative teaching environment that is being developed in P-12 schools, teacher candidates also must be better prepared in the needed interpersonal skills such as respecting the viewpoint of others, maintaining an open attitude to new ideas, or simply being able to accept the values of others. Teacher candidates need time to develop and practice these skills.

PROFESSIONAL LEARNING COMMUNITIES

A belief that individuals who share common goals can learn from each other within a framework that encourages collaboration underlies professional learning communities (Lieberman & Miller, 2011; Renfro, 2007). As teaching has shifted from a focus on assuring that students are taught to a focus on assuring that students learn, professional learning communities have emerged as an environment that can best prepare future teachers to develop the pedagogical strategies needed to attain that end.

A professional learning community has been characterized by Dufour (2004) as providing both strong collaboration and a focused effort to improve practice. There is a difference between a professional learning community and simply a team that may choose to meet at random or regular times for a specific purpose. The unique characteristics of a professional learning community are the collaborative culture that surrounds the community and the shared commitment to not only learner outcomes but also reflective practice.

Learning communities facilitate the creation of collaborative relationships that not only can focus on student learning outcomes but also can address the sense of isolation that may arise in beginning teachers. In creating professional learning communities, the concept of teaching as solo practice is replaced with teaching within a collegial and collaborative environment. An integrated professional environment that links novice teachers and more experienced educators in providing support for responsibilities may alleviate the sense of isolation felt by new teachers (Kardos & Johnson, 2007).

Although the focus of a professional learning community is student learning, teacher reflection is an embedded part of the process. The outcomes of strong partnerships may make conversations that have previously been private become shared. Educators may need additional training and support in establishing a comfortable process of working together. Teamwork doesn't come easily and requires more than school and district verbal support; collaboration takes time and directed effort to provide opportunities for teachers to truly engage with each other (Dufour, 2008; Renfro, 2007).

A community of practice that consists of both experienced and less experienced teachers is beneficial at all stages of teaching. Preservice teachers gain insight from more experienced cooperating teachers and university supervisors. Induction-level teachers continue to develop the ability to reflect and improve their professional practice as they join veteran teachers in professional learning communities within their initial professional placements.

Although not new to teaching, veteran teachers can often learn new strategies from teacher candidates fresh from the classroom and bursting with new techniques they are eager to try. A professional learning community brings educators together and allows veteran teachers an opportunity to provide the modeling in the process of reflection from which teacher candidates and induction-level teachers can benefit (Jones, 2012).

Effective Interpersonal Communication Within a Professional Learning Community

An element of a professional learning community that has been identified but not widely studied is the need for trust and honest communication. Huffman (2003) reports on a 5-year study on creating professional learning communities within multiple schools and describes the differences between mature and less mature communities.

Mature communities embed the trust and effective dialogues that are needed for members to collaborate in a meaningful way to encourage enhanced learner outcomes, while less mature communities struggle with developing trustful relationships among members of the community.

Professional learning communities are not always fully aware of the interpersonal challenges of collaborative relationships among its members. In addition to the emotions that can arise from individual reflection on personal practices, the creation of a community itself may create new conflicts as educators share emotionally charged beliefs or values. Professional differences that emerge from individual teaching practices or values can evoke conflict or intense reactions (Dooner, Mandzuk, & Clifton, 2007).

Although professional learning communities are cooperative in intent, an element to overcome in effective collaboration within learning communities is that collegiality can be challenging to accomplish in real practice (Servage, 2008).

Reflecting on one's own practice can involve the emergence of change. Participants may experience strong responses while examining their own beliefs and practices in contrast to the beliefs and practices of others. He and Levin (2008) interviewed teacher candidates, cooperating teachers, and teacher educators regarding their personal beliefs across multiple topics.

The topics included teachers, instruction, the classroom, teaching and learning, students, and parents. Interview data suggested that teacher candidates, cooperating teachers, and university supervisors might hold different personal beliefs about all topics. The differences in personal beliefs can be an obstacle to communication if there are no opportunities for three-way conversations among the stakeholders.

Teacher habits of mind can also be a factor in establishing effective collaboration (Vescio, Ross, & Adams, 2008). Teachers come to the classroom with different levels of capability or commitment, and these can become relevant within the processes that inspire collaboration within learning communities. As a learning community strives to develop personal awareness of how awareness of one's own practice—more than general knowledge about teaching—directly affects student learning, the discovery of one's own habits of mind becomes a factor.

Professional Learning Communities During Student Teaching

In a personal account of his own experience as a teacher candidate, Miller (2008) suggested that a social context could be a beneficial environment for preservice teacher learning. He identified multiple dimensions in which this can occur, including the several ways in which new teachers or teacher candidates can explore their own beliefs and practices. Professional learning communities provide the opportunity to receive the professional support and encouragement that can counter feelings of isolation in developing personal teaching practices.

Yet understanding the interpersonal aspect of collaboration may be a vital element that is missing in preservice teacher experiences because it is often overlooked as a factor. Differences in beliefs or values in themselves do not present a barrier to effective collaboration; however, the fact that differences may exist seems to give additional evidence to the importance of open and ongoing communication.

Student teachers or interns who may have not yet acquired collaborative skills and ways to reflect on their own or within a learning community of others may be provided their first opportunity to learn and practice in a directed way during student teaching. Bond (2013) has noted that teachers who are new to participation in learning communities may tend to focus on themselves rather than their students. As a result, interpersonal conflicts among members of a learning community can arise.

What better opportunity to participate in an initial professional learning community than during student teaching where an ongoing three-way relationship among the teacher candidate, the supervising classroom teacher, and the university supervisor has already been created? The creation of an initial professional learning community among these three individuals becomes a viable and beneficial way to provide opportunities for the teacher candidate to develop the needed knowledge, skills, and dispositions to participate productively within a collaborative professional culture.

Models of Professional Learning Communities

An example of a professional learning community that has been used effectively with teacher candidates to create a bridge between practitioners and teacher candidates was developed at Samford University (Hoaglund et al., 2014). The educator preparation program developed teacher candidate professional learning communities during three semesters before student teaching within teaching methods courses.

Each group included a faculty member. A collaborative culture was developed among the teacher candidates within student learning communities that subsequently transitioned into membership in professional learning communities at their partner schools when placed in K-12 classrooms.

The Preservice Teacher Institute (PTI) at the University of South Alabama was developed for senior elementary education candidates as well as faculty mentors during a semester of student teaching. Teacher candidates and experienced facilitators engaged in PTI seminars focused on specific topics at the same time as the candidates' classroom placements. The seminars provided a comfortable environment in which teacher candidates could make interpersonal connections with experienced teachers and could engage in more reflective dialogues (Kent & Simpson, 2009).

Rowan University provided a semester-long learning community opportunity for its teacher education candidates at the earliest stages (Meredith, 2010). A course addressing learning communities was paired with participation in urban elementary school classrooms and active collaboration with classroom teachers. The classroom teachers became learning partners with the teacher candidates and were able to share their knowledge of factors relevant to student learning in urban schools.

The Partnership Learning Triangle (Rigelman & Ruben, 2012) is another approach to devising collaboration between K-8 schools and an educator preparation program. The core of the Partnership Learning Triangle was multiple levels of collaboration within school and university partnerships. Within an equilateral triad model, teacher candidates interacted with each other, K-8 teachers, and other educator preparation faculty.

Collaboration and collegiality was more readily encouraged than within more typical hierarchical connections. Within the triad, teacher candidates could learn relevant teaching skills from each other, teacher mentors, or university faculty. Even more importantly, all members developed an effective collaborative mind-set that facilitated the reflective dialogues that can enhance student learning.

The ability to evaluate student understanding collaboratively with peers is a prerequisite skill to collaboration (Santagata & Guarino, 2012). A group of 40 preservice teachers' awareness and knowledge of collaboration during math methods instruction paired with clinical placements indicated that teacher candidate awareness of collaboration varied among the 40 candidates.

Teacher candidates who do not begin with the ability to collaborate effectively could improve through opportunities to do so in structured environments. The authors suggested that if educator preparation programs provided earlier opportunities for candidate interaction with other professionals, more highly developed collaborative skills might emerge within teacher candidates upon program completion.

The Role of the University Supervisor

There may be differences among university supervisors in critical reflection skills, as some may have recently moved from teaching roles to supervisory roles and may not be accustomed to actively reflecting on their own teaching beliefs and expressing it to adult learners (Bates et al., 2009). For others, especially university faculty, it may be an already-developed process.

Because critical reflection is a developing skill in teacher candidates, a university supervisor has a unique opportunity to model and encourage the process of critical reflection during student teaching supervision. University supervisors can initially provide examples of an awareness of their own beliefs through thoughtful discussions with teacher candidates.

They gradually can become listeners as candidates learn to identify and articulate their own beliefs about teaching while engaged in the day-to-day opportunities for reflection that student teaching provides. University supervisors also have an opportunity to identify and support the teacher dispositions needed by teacher candidates for effective collaboration and participation in professional learning communities.

The Role of the Cooperating Teacher

Classroom teachers serve as mentors to teacher candidates in ways the university supervisor cannot accomplish. Grossman (2010) and Feiman-Nemser (1998) found that the most effective mentors have had experience with collaborative learning in some ways and have formulated clearer ideas about their own practices. Experienced teachers have a major role in educator preparation, not just by making their classrooms available for clinical placement, but also by sharing their experience and modeling their skills.

Although classroom teachers report that they enjoy working with teacher candidates, they also report challenges. Classroom teachers may not be eager to counsel candidates in problematic placement situations or spend the additional time needed to do so. They also report feeling less respected and recognized by university faculty (Bullough et al., 2004). Once again, as a collaborative culture is better and more fully developed within educator preparation programs, the interpersonal aspects of a successful collaborative process can become better recognized and more appropriately addressed.

PREPARING TEACHER CANDIDATES FOR A COLLABORATIVE PROFESSIONAL CULTURE

Educator preparation programs don't currently prepare preservice teachers to develop effective communication skills (Lawley et al., 2014). In creating a collaborative professional culture within teaching, all teacher educators must model the skills and dispositions that reflect a collegial environment as an irrefutable element of accomplished and effective teaching (Aleccia, 2011).

Current P-12 teachers can be the voices for what is missing in educator preparation. They have informed us that some programs do not provide student teaching experiences that reflect the demands of 21st-century teaching. Today's teachers report a need to learn within a collaborative learning community and to reflect together as they try to meet the needs of their students (Chesley & Jordan, 2012; Jones, 2012). They want to learn within a community of practice.

Mentoring during teacher induction is a way to provide teacher support but remains a model that focuses on matching new teachers with veteran teachers. This system still fosters more of a solo approach to teaching rather than provide a fuller environment of collaboration with more than just one mentor (Goodwin, 2012; Grossman & Davis, 2012; National Commission on Teaching and America's Future, 2005). Mentoring alone doesn't significantly reduce the number of educators leaving the profession and doesn't provide the sense of community support that new teachers say they need.

Teacher Residencies

Teacher residencies are being incorporated into educator preparation programs. The National Education Association (2014) developed a task force to evaluate the effectiveness of teacher residencies as a component of educator preparation. The task force carefully examined several educator preparation programs across the country that embodied active partnerships between university educator preparation programs and P-12 schools and characterized a residency as a partnership between educator program providers and the P-12 school districts and systems in which teacher candidates will complete clinical placements.

Residencies should focus on the integration of theory with practice and collaboration between experienced teachers and teacher candidates. A residency should encompass a collaborative culture in which both parties are actively engaged in preparation of teacher candidates who can demonstrate readiness for all aspects of teaching.

Teacher Performance Assessments

To assure that teacher candidates demonstrate professional readiness, teacher performance assessments are often incorporated into final clinical experiences. During my experience guiding student teachers through a performance-based assessment required for teacher certification over multiple semesters and also serving as a university supervisor for student teaching, I have noted that many of the benefits of a professional learning community emerge during the process.

Completion of a performance-based assessment such as the edTPA requires a teacher candidate to work collaboratively with the classroom teacher in whose classroom the edTPA tasks must be completed and the university supervisor whose expertise in the assessment is welcomed. The focus of the collaboration is on positive student outcomes, as this is the goal of a teacher performance-based assessment.

Successful completion of the edTPA requires careful lesson planning, thorough assessment, effective teaching, and careful reflection on all elements of teaching. In supporting teacher candidates through the assessment process, both the classroom teacher and university supervisor naturally engage in multiple collaborative conversations regarding the candidate's teaching.

The future of teacher education includes performance assessments completed during student teaching. Performance assessments that clearly focus on student learning outcomes and reflective practice are useful to students as they transition into the induction phase of teaching. They can serve as a catalyst for collaboration among the candidate, the classroom teacher upon whose students the candidate is focusing during completion of the assessment, and the university supervisor who is guiding the candidate in completion of the performance assessment.

They can provide a framework to create a professional learning community in which a candidate can truly focus on student learning. In addition, they can further provide a structure in which the interpersonal skills needed to collaborate with others can blossom as the candidate learns the skills of reflective practice and sharing that practice with others.

REFERENCES

Aleccia, V. (2011). Walking our talk: The imperative of teacher education modeling. *The Clearing House, 84*, 87–90. doi: 10.1080/00098655.2010.524951

Association of Teacher Educators. (n.d.a). Standards for teacher educators. Retrieved from http://www.ate1.org/pubs/uploads/tchredstds0308.pdf

Association of Teacher Educators. (n.d.b). Why the standards. Retrieved from http://www.ate1.org/pubs/Why_the_Standards.cfm

Bates, A.J., Ramirez, L., & Drits, D. (2009). Connecting university supervision and critical reflection: Mentoring and modeling. *The Teacher Educator, 44*(2), 90–112. doi: 10.1080/08878730902751993

Bond, N. (2013). Developing a professional learning community among preservice teachers. *Current Issues in Education, 16*(2), 1–14. Retrieved from http://cie.asu.edu/ojs/index.php/cieatasu/index

Bullough, R.V., Draper, R.J., Smith, L., & Birrell, J. (2004). Moving beyond collusion: Clinical faculty and university/public school partnership. *Teaching and Teacher Education, 20*, 505–552. doi:10.1016/j.tate.2004.04.007

Chesley, G.M., & Jordan, J. (2012). What's missing from teacher prep. *Educational Leadership, 69*(8), 41–45. Retrieved from http://www.ascd.org/publications/educational-leadership.aspx

Council for the Accreditation of Educator Preparation. (2015). The CAEP standards. Retrieved from http://caepnet.org/standards/introduction

Council of Chief State School Officers. (2013). InTASC model core teaching standards and learning progress for teachers 1.0. Retrieved from http://www.ccsso.org/resources/publications/InTasc_model_core_teaching_standards_and_learning_progressions_for_teachers_10.html

Dooner, A., Mandzak, D., & Clifton, R.A. (2007). Stages of collaboration and the realities of professional learning communities. *Teaching and Teacher Education, 24*, 564–574. doi:10.1016/j.tate.2007.09.009

DuFour, R. (2004). What is a professional learning community? *Educational Leadership, 61*(8), 6–11. Retrieved from http://www.ascd.org/publications/educational-leadership.aspx

Feiman-Nemser, S. (1998). Teachers as teacher educators. *European Journal of Teacher Education, 21*(1), 63–74. doi:10.1080/0261976980210107

Feiman-Nemser, S. (2012). Beyond solo teaching. *Educational Leadership, 69*(8), 10–16. Retrieved from http://www.ascd.org/publications/educational-leadership.aspx

Goodwin, B. (2012). New teachers face three common challenges. *Educational Leadership, 69*(8), 84–85. Retrieved from http://www.ascd.org/publications/educational-leadership.aspx

Grossman, P. (2010). *Learning to practice: The design of clinical experience in teacher preparation* (Policy Brief). Retrieved from http://www.nea.org/assets/docs/Clinical_Experience_-_Pam_Grossman.pdf

Grossman, P., & Davis, E. (2012). Mentoring that fits. *Educational Leadership, 69*(8), 54–57. Retrieved from http://www.ascd.org/publications/educational-leadership.aspx

He, Y., & Levin, B.B. (2008). Match or mismatch? How congruent are the beliefs of teacher candidates, cooperating teachers, and university-based teacher educators? *Teacher Education Quarterly, 35*(4), 37–55. Retrieved from http://www.teqjournal.org/

Hoaglund, A.E., Birkenfeld, K., & Box, J.A. (2014). Professional learning communities: Creating a foundation for collaboration skills in pre-service teachers. *Education, 134*(4), 521–528. Retrieved from http://www.projectinnovation.com/education.html

Huffman, J. (2003). The role of shared values and vision in creating professional learning communities. *NASSP Bulletin, 87*(637), 21–32. doi:10.1177/019263650308763703

Jones, B.K. (2012). A new teacher's plea. *Educational Leadership, 69*(8), 74–77. Retrieved from http://www.ascd.org/publications/educational-leadership.aspx

Kardos, S.M., & Johnson, S.M. (2007). On their own and presumed expert: New teachers' experience with their colleagues. *Teachers College Record, 109*(9), 2083–2106. Retrieved from http://www.tcrecord.org

Kent, A.M., & Simpson, J. (2009). Preservice teacher institute: Developing a model learning community for student teachers. *College Student Journal, 43*(2), 695–704. Retrieved from http://www.projectinnovation.com/college-student-journal.html

Korth, B.B., Erickson, L., & Hall, K.M. (2009). Defining teacher educator through the eyes of classroom teachers. *The Professional Educator, 33*(1), 16–27. Retrieved from http://wp.auburn.edu/educate/

Lawley, J.J., Moore, J., & Smajik, A. (2014). Effective communication between preservice and cooperating teachers. *The New Educator, 10*(2), 153–162. doi: 10.1080/1547688X.2014.898495

Lieberman, A., & Miller, L. (2011). Learning communities: The starting point for professional learning is in schools and classrooms. *JSD, 32*(4), 16–20. Retrieved from http://learningforward.org/publications/jsd#.VsPFGFLo0qM

Meredith, C.C. (2010). Applied learning in teacher education: Learning communities among pre-service candidates and urban elementary schools. *The Journal of Human Resources and Adult Learning, 6*(2), 80–85. Retrieved from http://www.hraljournal.com/index.htm

Miller, M. (2008). Problem-based conversations: Using preservice teachers problems as a mechanism for their professional development. *Teacher Education Quarterly, 35*(4), 77–98. Retrieved from http://www.teqjournal.org

National Commission on Teaching and America's Future. (2003). No dream denied: A pledge to America's children. Retrieved from http://nctaf.org/wp-content/uploads/no-dream-denied_summary_report.pdf

National Commission on Teaching and America's Future. (2005). Induction into learning communities. Retrieved from http://files.eric.ed.gov/fulltext/ED494581.pdf

National Education Association. (2014). Teacher residencies: Redefining preparation through Partnerships (NEA Report). Retrieved from https://www.nea.org/assets/docs/Teacher-Residencies-2014.pdf

Renfro, E.R. (2007). Professional learning communities impact student success. *Leadership Compass, 5*(2), 1–3.

Rigelman, N.M., & Ruben, B. (2012). Creating foundations for collaboration in schools: Utilizing professional learning communities to support teacher candidate learning and visions of teaching. *Teaching and Teacher Education, 28*, 979–989. doi:10.1016/j.tate.2012.05.004

Santagata, R., & Guarino, J. (2012). Preparing future teachers to collaborate. *Issues in Teacher Education, 21*(1), 59–69. Retrieved from http://www1.chapman.edu/ITE/index.html

Scherer, L. (2012). The challenges of supporting new teachers. *Educational Leadership, 69*(8), 18–23. Retrieved from http://www.ascd.org/publications/educational-leadership.aspx

Servage, L. (2008). Critical and transformative practices in professional learning communities. *Teacher Education Quarterly, 35*(1), 63–77. Retrieved from http://www.teqjournal.org/

Vescio, V., Ross, D., & Adams, A. (2008). A review of research on the impact of professional learning communities on teaching practice and student learning. *Teaching and Teacher Education, 24*, 80–91. doi:10.1016/j.tate.2007.01.004

Chapter Five

Critical Understandings of Classroom Teachers as Associated Teacher Educators on Learning in Landscapes of Practice

A Case Study Approach

Sandra L. Hardy and Caroline M. Crawford

ABSTRACT

Learning communities and field-based, embedded teacher education programs of study naturally support the concept of learning communities bound within landscapes of practice and engagement. The vitality and collegial efforts support the teacher candidate's knowledge acquisition while engaging in real-world, field-based efforts; yet also of vital importance is the embedding of the teacher candidates within real-world practical environments so as to ease the integrational understandings of teacher candidates into the professional education community. As such, the critical understandings and viewpoints connected with classroom teachers as associated teacher educators are brought forward and explored. Within this discussion, highlighted are major themes that evolved from a qualitative review of classroom teacher comments that revolve around three research questions.

KEYWORDS

case study, classroom teacher, landscapes of practice, learning, learning community, novice classroom teacher, university faculty, veteran classroom teacher

CRITICAL UNDERSTANDINGS OF CLASSROOM TEACHERS AS ASSOCIATED TEACHER EDUCATORS ON LEARNING IN LANDSCAPES OF PRACTICE: A CASE STUDY APPROACH

An interesting discussion that began early in 2013 at the founding of the Association of Teacher Educators' (ATE) Commission on Classroom Teachers as Associated Teacher Educators introduced four simple questions revolving around perceptions of classroom teachers as focused upon field-based teacher education programs of study. The resulting research has offered significant support and enriched understandings of the developing perceptions and conceptual comprehensions of classroom teachers as associated teacher educators.

Professional discourse revealed areas for further exploration framed around unsolicited responses to four primary areas of interest. These areas of the commission's dialogue thus became the four guiding research questions which resulted in the study effort and findings to follow.

PURPOSE

The purpose of this case study approach was to further expand the professional knowledge base of the field-based understandings pertaining to classroom teachers engaged in supporting field-based teacher education programs of study. Furthermore, this research sought to examine novice classroom teachers beginning their career paths within the realms of elementary and secondary classroom teaching.

SIGNIFICANCE

The significance of this study effort directs in advancing the understandings and the perceptions of elementary and secondary classroom teachers who are engaged in professional and collegial interchanges that revolve around classroom teachers as associated teacher educators within traditional field-based teacher education programs of study. Further in importance are the forthcoming and integral implications consistent with comprehensive support of novice teachers.

The high quality of engagement throughout the field-based teacher education programs of study emphasizes the collegial relationships and voice associated with openness and comfort level among the different yet integrated and inherently necessary roles of professionals.

The resulting dynamic creates a stronger and transparent understanding of respectful approaches associated with the education of teacher candidates within the field environment. The critical impact of classroom teachers as associated teacher educators is clearly influential and necessary toward the teacher candidate success and stands to promote the practice of professional teacher educator standards.

STANDARDS FOR TEACHER EDUCATORS

The Association of Teacher Educators' Standards for Teacher Educators (ATE, n.d.) reflect upon the dispositional levels of engagement, understanding, and indicators that more fully embrace the realm of teacher educators. Throughout this initial foray into the presentation of burgeoning themes and subthemes that arose from this qualitative analysis of the data, the manuscript embeds an understanding of the following nine standards: STANDARD 1—Teaching; STANDARD 2—Cultural Competence; STANDARD 3—Scholarship; STANDARD 4—Professional Development; STANDARD 5—Program Development; STANDARD 6—Collaboration; STANDARD 7—Public Advocacy; STANDARD 8—Teacher Education Profession; and STANDARD 9—Vision (ATE, n.d., pp. 1–8).

COMMUNITY ENGAGEMENT: LEARNING IN LANDSCAPES OF PRACTICE

Communities of engagement have been recognized as meaningful and appropriate within successful professional environments. Initially the concept of learning communities delved into concepts of successful engagement throughout the instructional process. Wenger's work (1998, 2009) enriched further into the concept by framing communities of practice as social engagement within the professional realm and as people coming together for specific purposes and goals. Of interest is Wenger's (1998) statement, "So, what if we adopted a different perspective, one that placed learning in the context of our lived experience of participation in the world?" (p. 3; Wenger, 2009, p. 210), leading to a more holistic and participatory experience that beautifully parallels the more recent Wenger-Trayner, Fenton-O'Creevy, Hutchinson, Kubiak, and Wenger-Trayner (2015) reconceptualization of learning in landscapes of practice.

This metaphoric representation of a professional community that engages in field-specific practices is integrally important as associated with field-based teacher education programs of study due to the inherent environmental impact of the site-based practices and communications that support the teacher candidate. More fully reflective of this study is the recognition of the fundamental importance and influence of classroom teachers who are also associated teacher educators, working alongside university faculty and teacher candidates toward the *onboarding* or *credentialing* of teachers.

Specifically these efforts lean toward orienting or familiarizing teacher candidates with the site-based real-world understanding of classroom teacher responsibilities, expectations, nuances, and real-world career depth and breadth of engagement. Based upon the significance of classroom teachers as associated teacher candidates within the learning communities of practice, it is necessary and appropriate to develop a snapshot of understanding that is reflective of classroom teachers engaged in the teacher education process.

FRAMING THE ENVIRONMENT

This study occurred in the suburban school districts that surround a large metropolitan area, within the southern United States of America. Worthy of mention is that the school districts throughout this regional area are not union-based and are bound within a right to work state. Two school districts were included within the scope of this study, including elementary school and secondary school sites.

PARTICIPANTS

A total of 32 classroom teachers voluntarily participated in a brief open-ended list of questions. Out of the 32 classroom teachers who participated, 8 provided their years of experience as a classroom teacher, reflecting a range of classroom teaching experience from 7 to 28 years. The subjects taught by the participants were revealed by 20 of the 32 respondents that also included a total of 5 coaches: three soccer coaches, one football coach, and one basketball coach who also taught chemistry.

RESEARCH QUESTIONS

The four research questions were framed as open-ended questions to promote elaboration of responses offered by participants. The four research questions were stated as follows:

RQ 1: What would classroom teachers want university supervisors to know?
RQ 2: What would veteran classroom educators want novice classroom educators to know?
RQ 3: What are important qualities/components of teacher leaders that are necessary to support novice teachers?
RQ 4: What would novice classroom teachers want veteran classroom teacher educators to know?

The focus of this study was intriguing based on the professional discursive communicative effort extended toward more fully understanding classroom teachers' discourse and reflections when requested to respond to specified open-ended questions (Stake, 1995, 2005).

DATA ANALYSIS

An analysis of the data subgroups based on content area taught was compared and contrasted for each research question. The years of teaching experience are listed prior to the verbatim quotations for those respondents who provided such information, to reflect years of experience upon which the statement may be based. The data were analyzed through emergent patterns pertaining to each research question within and across participant subgroups. The analysis focused upon a presentation of the data as verbatim quotations that were organized into six subgroups derived from classroom teachers' content area taught.

FINDINGS

The presentation of findings within this section focused initially upon the specific participant quotations. The next area of focus within each research question findings discussion was the analysis of the subgroups for the designated research question.

Research Question One Findings

The research question focused upon within this section is Research Question One: What would classroom teachers want university supervisors to know? The participant quotations are offered as an initial presentation of understanding, directly followed by an analysis of the subgroups.

Participant quotations. The participant quotations are offered as responses to Research Question One. Please reflect upon the framing of the quotations within school site and subject contracted to teach. The school site participants who responded to this question include elementary teachers and pre-school teacher, English teachers, Spanish teachers, science teachers, math teacher, history teachers, vocational education style classes, and coaches. Table 5.1 presents quoted responses to Research Question One, from elementary classroom teachers and a PPCD classroom teacher for a pre-school program for children with disabilities.

Table 5.2 focuses upon a presentation of quotation responses to Research Question One, from high school English and Spanish classroom teachers.

Table 5.1. Research Question One Quotations: Elementary Teachers and Pre-School Teacher

Subject Contracted to Teach	Years	Subject Taught/Quotation
PPCD Teacher for Preschool Program for Children with Disabilities		"She would want them to know that the lesson plans" "Teachers today are nothing like the ones we were taught to do in school. She does however think it's helpful to do long lengthy lessons required in college to help learn to think through a complete lesson cycle."
Kindergarten		"I would want professors to know that teaching is a very hard but rewarding field."
Kindergarten		"Mrs. _____ would like to thank her professors because without them she wouldn't have become a teacher."
First Grade		"The most valuable assignments I had in college were the actual interactions with students. We went to schools and were able to work with small groups of students of different grade levels."
Fourth Grade	28	"New teachers need frequent visits and immediate feedback in regards to their lesson planning, classroom management and ability to impart knowledge to their students. Giving an area of focus can help the teacher analyze their impact on student learning."

Table 5.2. Research Question One Quotations: High School English and Spanish Teachers

Subject Contracted to Teach	Years	Subject Taught/Quotation
English IV/AP		"I'd like university professors to know that today's students are diverse learners. We no longer operate in an educational system in which everyone sits in rows, takes notes, and regurgitates knowledge. Our students are knowledgeable and capable, but they are used to operating as problem solvers, not databases, and instruction should take advantage of those strengths such as felicity with technology, fluent communication, interpersonal negotiation, and the use of every hour of the day."
English	27	"That we are trying, but forces outside the classroom are hindering our effectiveness. Students' accountability is almost nonexistent."
English III		"University supervisors should know that modern students expect a modern classroom."

Subject Contracted to Teach	Years	Subject Taught/Quotation
English	7	"That more lessons on classroom management would be nice."
Spanish		"Classroom teachers would probably want university professors to know that what is taught in the education field is only the ideal picture of a classroom. Teachers in the classroom experience real life situations that sometimes do not match up to what is taught when taking an education course at the university. Being flexible is a must."
Spanish		"That most students coming into a university don't know how to use PowerPoint, Hakudeck, and Prezi."

Table 5.3. Research Question One Quotations: High School Science, Math and History Teachers

Subject Contracted to Teach	Years	Subject Taught/Quotation
Anatomy		"Students are used to having many opportunities to improve their grades. This is very different from college."
Chemistry, Football and Basketball Coach	7	"Classroom teachers would want professors to know the types of students they are getting. They need to be informed about their attentiveness, study habits, and different ways to keep them engaged in class."
Math	12	"He would want his university professor to know that he wants to be a teacher. The professor should know the factors that affect him as a student teacher, whether it's the fact he has a job or is even a single parent."
History, Soccer Coach		"Wants them to know that there are different students that have different learning styles."
History		"University supervisors should know that the world of education is becoming much more technological. It would be a good thing to start showing teacher candidates ways of incorporating technology into the classroom."

Table 5.3 focuses upon a presentation of quotation responses to Research Question One, from high school Science, Math and History classroom teachers.

Table 5.4 focuses upon a presentation of quotation responses to Research Question One, from high school vocational education and coach/classroom teachers.

Table 5.4. Research Question One Quotations: High School Vocational Education and Coach Teachers

Subject Contracted to Teach	Years	Subject Taught/Quotation
JROTC		"How prepared the students are for college level classes. And, students are eager to learn at a higher level."
Career and Technical	13	"She would want for university supervisors to understand that it's not how it used to be, because of technology. . . . "
Coach		"Wants them to know that there are different students that have different learning styles."
Football and Basketball Coach, Chemistry Teacher	7	"Classroom teachers would want professors to know the type of students they are getting. They need to be informed about their attentiveness, study habits, and different ways to keep them engaged in class."
Football/Basketball, Chemistry	7	"That all students are not created equal. Each student has a unique learning style."
Girls' Soccer Coach	16	"Professors should know students work ethic, knowledge of the subject, and ability to understand concepts and theories."

Analysis of the Subgroups

It is interesting to note that three of the seven subgroups (elementary/preschool teachers, English teachers, and coaches) had expressed common ideas within their respective subgroup concerning what classroom teachers would want university supervisors to know. Three of the five teachers in the elementary/preschool subgroup noted the importance of the clinical aspect of learning to teach in clinical settings supported by university professors in the schools' classrooms.

The relevance of university coursework to clinical collaborations was also highlighted. Three of the four English teachers indicated the need for university supervisors to know "times have changed." These classroom teachers as teacher educators illuminated the need for enhanced awareness on the part of university professors as to the realities of the clinical classroom setting. The coaches' responses reflected the importance of knowing each student as a unique individual learner.

Similar to the English teachers' replies, the coaches echoed their perception which reflected that university professors were not as informed as they need to be about the reality of students in the classrooms outside of the university. No patterns were found within the other subgroups. There were also no patterns discovered in regards to the responses and years of teaching experience.

The patterns that emerged in the analysis of data suggested elementary teachers, English teachers, and coaches classroom viewed the role of university professor in the classroom of K-12 teachers as in need of providing better support for classroom teachers as teacher educators.

In summary, three of the seven subgroups had patterns in their responses that were clustered to express classroom teachers' perceptions that university professors need to be more informed about the realities of the clinical setting in schools to best meet the needs of students and teachers. Furthermore, the respondents indicated that university professors needed to know their value in connecting university course work to clinical experiences and provide the supportive feedback in the process required to make such an exchange meaningful and effective.

Research Question Two Findings

The research question focused upon within this section is Research Question Two: What would veteran classroom educators want novice classroom educators to know? The participant quotations are offered as an initial presentation of understanding prior to an analysis of the subgroups.

Participant quotations. The following are the participant quotations offered as responses to Research Question Two. Please reflect upon the framing of the quotations within school site and subject contracted to teach. The school site participants who responded to this question include elementary teachers and pre-school teacher, English teachers, Spanish teachers, science teachers, math teacher, history teachers, vocational education style classes, and coaches. Table 5.5 presents quoted responses to Research Question Two, from elementary classroom teachers and a PPCD classroom teacher for a preschool program for children with disabilities.

Table 5.6 highlights quotation responses to Research Question Two, from high school English and Spanish classroom teachers.

Table 5.7 focuses upon a presentation of quotation responses to Research Question Two, from high school science, math, and history classroom teachers.

Table 5.8 focuses upon a presentation of quotation responses to Research Question Two, from high school vocational education and coach/classroom teachers.

Analysis of the subgroups. Three of the elementary teachers indicated in their responses that veteran teachers would want novice teacher to know that teaching is difficult. This was interpreted from the following phrases in the replies: "teaching is hard." The subphrases that were interpreted were "know

Table 5.5. Research Question Two Quotations: Elementary Teachers and Pre-School Teacher

Subject Contracted to Teach	Years	Subject Taught/Quotation
PPCD Teacher for Preschool Program for Children with Disabilities		"She would want them to know that teaching is not an easy job. People don't become teachers for the salary. You will be underpaid and under-appreciated, but what you gain from it personally is worth much more than any amount of money you could ever receive."
Kindergarten		"I would want them to know that teaching is not easy! You have to be very flexible and you need to be caring but firm, and you need to have good classroom management."
Kindergarten		"A few tips Mrs. _____ would want to give candidates is that it will be tough at the beginning but patients is the key."
First Grade		"Be organized! Have it clear in your mind how the lesson/activity will go prior to starting it. You cannot state your expectations too many times."
Fourth Grade	28	"Ask for help from supervisors and veteran teachers. Be willing to accept help, as well as criticism. Teaching is hard! Most often, people skills are more important than knowledge of content. Building relationships with students is necessary before they will want to learn from you."

Table 5.6. Research Question Two Quotations: High School English and Spanish Teachers

Subject Contracted to Teach	Years	Subject Taught/Quotation
English IV/AP		"One thing that many novice teachers don't realize is that student discussion is a powerful tool. Students are energetic and inclined to use that energy amongst one another. If that energy can be harnessed, not suppressed, it can provide the fuel and power for learning. Silencing students is more work for less return. Using their own excitement for instructional purposes builds a strongly collegial, affective learning environment."
English	27	"Get through the bs any way you can and find your own voice. Be passionate for kids, not so much subject."
English III		"Novice classroom educators should know that students need to learn how to find information and apply what they learn."
English	7	"To be prepared that teaching is not an easy profession."

Subject Contracted to Teach	Years	Subject Taught/Quotation
Spanish		"Classroom teachers would want teacher candidates to know that teaching requires time, a lot of work, and patience with students and oneself. Also, new teachers should understand that lesson plans that may have been put into place with ample time will most likely change according to the needs of the students; this is normal and one should adjust and be flexible."
Spanish		"That students need second chances."

Table 5.7. Research Question Two Quotations: High School Science, Math and History Teachers

Subject Contracted to Teach	Years	Subject Taught/Quotation
Anatomy		"It's ok to be stressed and feel like you are failing. It will get better. Give it a few months to years."
Chemistry, Football and Basketball Coach	7	"Classroom teachers would want novice teachers to know what to expect from students in the classroom. They need to be informed about how to manipulate the curriculum to assist students in a better understanding of the material. Teaching strategies should be discussed by both the veteran and novice teachers to help each other bring out the best in their students."
Math	12	"He would want novice classroom educators to know that not everything is the end of the world. There will be problems occurring daily, adjust to those problems and move on. Things will get better with time and experience."
History and Soccer Coach		"Having to adapt and willing to make changes to your lesson plan."
History		"Whatever your plan is for classroom management, double the intensity of it your first year. It will keep you more sane."

Table 5.8. Research Question Two Quotations: High School Vocational Education and Coach Teachers

Subject Contracted to Teach	Years	Subject Taught/Quotation
JROTC		"That students are students and should be treated as young adults and respect them and treat them as young adults."

(Continued)

Table 5.8. Continued

Subject Contracted to Teach	Years	Subject Taught/Quotation
Career and Technical	13	"She would like for novice classroom educators to know that it could be overwhelming and to be able to make it through the first year."
Soccer Coach & History Teacher		"Having to adapt and willing to make changes to your lesson plan."
Chemistry, Football and Basketball	7	"Classroom teachers would want novice classroom to know what to expect from students in the classroom. They need to be informed about how to manipulate the curriculum to assist students in a better understanding of the material. Teaching strategies should be discussed by both the veteran and novice teachers to help each other bring out the best in their students."
Varsity Soccer Coach		"Know that the better classroom management they have the better it will be to teach their subject."
Girls' Soccer Coach	16	"Novice teachers should be able to deal with everything going on in class such as many distractions."

that teaching is not an easy job," "know that teaching is not easy," and "teaching is hard!"

Three of the elementary teachers expressed that veteran teachers would want novice teachers to know about classroom management. "You need to have good classroom management." "Patients is key." "You cannot state your expectations too many times." "Building relationships with students is necessary . . ."

The English and Spanish teachers reflected similar thoughts, but the message was in bits rather than in clusters. "Using their own excitement for instructional purposes builds a strongly collegial \, affective learning environment." This statement suggests classroom management through instructional practices. "To be prepared that teaching is not an easy profession." This response pattern was also found in the elementary teachers' replies that teaching is difficult, "Students need second chances." This could also indicate classroom management as an important skill that veteran classroom teachers would want novice teachers to know.

Similar to the English and elementary teacher, the science and math teachers' responses revealed patterns of veteran classroom teachers wanting novice teachers to know teaching is challenging. But it will be better with time. "It's ok to be stressed and feel like you are failing. It will get better." ". . . not everything is the end of the world. . . . things will get better with time and experience."

Both history teachers emphasized the importance of being flexible. No patterns were found in the vocational education responses. One vocation education teacher emphasized the challenge of teaching. The other teacher shared the importance of respecting students. Respecting students applies to classroom management and also to instruction.

Three of the responses from the coaches reflected veteran teachers wanting novice teachers to know the important of flexibility. "Having to adapt and willing to make changes to your lesson plan." ". . . how to manipulate the curriculum . . .," ". . . be able to deal with everything going on in class such as many distractions."

To summarize, the elementary, Spanish, math, and science teachers all emphasized the message that teaching is difficult in response to what they thought veteran teachers would want novice teachers to know. The history teachers and coaches emphasized that veteran teachers would want novice teachers to know that flexibility is critical.

Research Question Three Findings

The research question focused upon within this section is Research Question Three: What are important qualities/components of teacher leaders that are necessary to support novice teachers? The participant quotations are offered as an initial presentation of understanding, directly followed by an analysis of the subgroups.

Participant quotations. Following are the participant quotations offered as responses to Research Question Three. Please reflect upon the framing of the quotations within school site and subject contracted to teach. The school site participants who responded to this question include elementary teachers and pre-school teacher, English teachers, Spanish teachers, science teachers, math teacher, history teachers, vocational education style classes, and coaches. Table 5.9 presents quoted responses to Research Question Three, from elementary classroom teachers and a PPCD classroom teacher for a pre-school program for children with disabilities.

Table 5.10 focuses upon a presentation of quotation responses to Research Question Three, from high school English and Spanish classroom teachers.

Table 5.11 focuses upon a presentation of quotation responses to Research Question Three, from high school Science, Math and History classroom teachers.

Table 5.12 focuses upon a presentation of quotation responses to Research Question Three, from high school vocational education and coach classroom teachers.

Analysis of the subgroups. Analysis of the subgroups responses to the third research question, "What are important qualities/components of teacher

Table 5.9. Research Question Three Quotations: Elementary Teachers and Pre-School Teacher

Subject Contracted to Teach	Years	Subject Taught/Quotation
PPCD Teacher for Preschool Program for Children with Disabilities		"Teacher leaders must be extremely organized, friendly, and are very patient."
Kindergarten		"Teacher preparation helps candidates develop the knowledge and skills needed in the classroom."
Kindergarten		"When mentoring another teacher one needs to be very patient and helpful and assist the teacher in any way they can. It's great if the new teacher can shadow the veteran teacher."
First Grade		"Be approachable, be realistic, be in constant contact with your teachers even if it is brief, be willing to share resources but also ask the newer teachers for ideas and input."
Fourth Grade	28	"Honesty, communication skills, confidence in the content area, commitment to lead by example, creative ability to address different learning styles, and the ability to inspire!"

Table 5.10. Research Question Three Quotations: High School English and Spanish Teachers

Subject Contracted to Teach	Years	Subject Taught/Quotation
English IV/AP	–	"Teacher leaders listen more than they speak, and they build on strength rather than working to eliminate weakness. Teaching is frustrating and can be disheartening, and often, teachers (especially novices) desperately need to feel heard and appreciated. It is not until someone feels valued that they can start to look at areas that might need growth; once strength is recognized, weakness can be addressed in a productive manner."
English	27	"Sense of humor! Not too far removed from the classroom . . . patience!"
English III		"Mentor teacher should be able to provide administrative support to the novice teachers."
English	7	"Compassionate, responsible, organized."
Spanish		"Teacher leaders can help novice teachers by being understanding and remember what it was like when they were in the classroom. Relating to new teachers and their feelings of being overwhelmed and stressed can help they feel that they have someone to turn to for help and advice."
Spanish		"That they are well organized, building relationships with the kids and they are lessons to real life."

Table 5.11. Research Question Three Quotations: High School Science, Math and History Teachers

Subject Contracted to Teach	Years	Subject Taught/Quotation
Anatomy		"Mentor means to be patient and be prepared to answer lots of questions. They also need to be able to give constructive criticism, without making the novice teacher feel inferior."
Chemistry, Football and Basketball Coach	7	"Teacher leaders need to help the novice teachers with materials, teaching strategies, and just being there to help at any time."
Math	12	"He thinks important qualities/ components that educators should have to be approachable, have experience, and be supportive."
History and Soccer Coach		"Someone that is knowledgeable and is willing to help."
History		"Compassion, availability, honesty. It's important to remember that the first year is the hardest year so don't 'sugar coat' things, be honest. It is also important to have the time to be a mentor. If you can't dedicate time to being there don't become one. Nothing is worse than battling the first year of teaching by yourself."

Table 5.12. Research Question Three Quotations: High School Vocational Education and Coach Teachers

Subject Contracted to Teach	Years	Subject Taught/Quotation
JROTC		"Willing to help others that are not as experienced caring about students and other teachers concerned about students getting a good education. Desire to see students succeed in high school and after school. Willing to work with students to help insure they learn."
Career and Technical Coordinator	13	"Important qualities/components of teacher leaders that are necessary to support novice teachers that for them to be good listeners and very, very positive and empathetic."
Soccer Coach and History Teacher		"Someone that is knowledgeable and is willing to help."
Football and Basketball Coach, Chemistry Teacher	7	"Teacher leaders need to help the novice teachers with materials, teaching strategies, and just being there to help at any time."
Varsity Soccer Coach		"Mentor teachers to share their experience and materials to help a new teacher be successful."
Girls' Soccer Coach	16	"Teacher leaders should show organization and be able to encourage learning."

100   *Chapter Five*

leaders that are necessary to support novice teachers?" uncovered the following patterns: The elementary teachers' responses revealed four of the teachers thought available support was an important quality of teacher leaders to support novice teachers.

Phrases are presented that were interpreted as available support: "constant contact," communication skills, "lead by example" were the phrases that were interpreted as available support. Two of the teachers emphasized patience as an important quality for teacher leaders. ". . . very patient. . .", ". . . very patient. . ." Similarly, the English and Spanish teachers also emphasized the importance of available support as a component of teacher leaders required to support novice teachers with phrases such as ". . . they build on strength," ". . . provide administrative support." "compassionate. . .," ". . . being understanding," and ". . . building relationships. . ."

Available support was also a common theme among science and math teachers: ". . . just being there to help any time," ". . . be approachable," and ". . . be patient. . . ." The teachers also had three replies that focused on knowledge as an important quality for teacher leaders to support novice teachers: ". . . answer lots of questions," "help at any time with materials, teaching strategies. . .," and "have experience and be supportive."

The history teachers also had evidence of the significant qualities of available support and knowledge. "Someone that is knowledgeable and is willing to help" and ". . . availability . . ." The vocational education teachers shared responses that reflected the qualities of availability and empathy. "Willing to help others . . .," Caring," ". . . concerned about students," "empathetic."

Patterns in the coaches' responses showed four responses of available support and four responses of the importance of knowledge as a quality for teacher leaders to support novice teachers. "Someone that is knowledgeable and willing to help," ". . . Help novice teachers with materials, teaching strategies, and just being there to help any time," . . . "share their experience and materials." The theme of available support as a key quality for teacher leaders to support novice teachers was found throughout all of the subgroups. Knowledge was also considered to be an important quality of teacher leaders followed by empathy.

Research Question Four Findings

The research question focused upon within this section is Research Question Four: What would novice classroom teachers want veteran classroom teacher educators to know? The participant quotations are offered as an initial presentation of understanding, directly followed by an analysis of the subgroups.

Participant quotations. Following are the participant quotations offered as responses to Research Question Four. Please reflect upon the framing of

Critical Understandings of Classroom Teachers as Associated Teacher   101

the quotations within school site and subject contracted to teach. The school site participants who responded to this question include elementary teachers and preschool teacher, English teachers, Spanish teachers, science teachers, math teacher, history teachers, vocational education-style classes, and coaches. Table 5.13 presents quoted responses to Research Question Four, from elementary classroom teachers and a PPCD classroom teacher for a preschool program for children with disabilities.

Table 5.14 focuses upon a presentation of quotation responses to Research Question Four, from high school English and Spanish classroom teachers.

Table 5.15 focuses upon a presentation of quotation responses to Research Question Four, from high school science, math, and history classroom teachers.

Table 5.16 focuses upon a presentation of quotation responses to Research Question Four, from high school vocational education and coach classroom teachers.

Table 5.13. Research Question Four Quotations: Elementary Teachers and Pre-School Teacher

Subject Contracted to Teach	Years	Subject Taught/Quotation
PPCD Teacher for Preschool Program for Children with Disabilities		"When she was a beginning teacher, she would want her mentor to know that some things seem easy to you, but she would need a little more time to get it together. She would tell them that she's sorry for asking so many questions and that she really appreciates all their time they give to help her."
Kindergarten	-	"I would think that new teachers would want veteran teachers to know that although they are new to the field that they have a lot of knowledge and creativity to offer."
Kindergarten	-	"Without veteran classroom teacher educators they wouldn't know as things and with their help the lessons will flow-by smoothly."
First Grade	-	"Their needs for further improvement, questions they might have, and to be respected as a teacher."
Fourth Grade	28	"Novice teachers need help! Most novice educators have content knowledge, but lack in the areas of classroom management and building relationships with students. Though these skills take time, most educators need additional help to get on the fast track to student achievement and success."

Table 5.14. Research Question Four Quotations: High School English and Spanish Teachers

Subject Contracted to Teach	Years	Subject Taught/Quotation
English IV/AP		"Novice teachers would want veteran teachers to know that they have something to offer despite inexperience. Those who are freshest out of school have had access to the newest techniques and research. They are the most energetic and on fire about the profession. Without new blood and new ideas, veteran teachers can become bitter and stagnant in a profession for which energy and innovation are vital."
English	27	"I need your input—but I am intimidated and overwhelmed."
English III		"Novice teachers might want veteran teachers to know that students need interaction and flexibility."
English	7	"That change is good."
Spanish		"New teachers would want veteran teachers to know that as times change, so does teaching. Teaching strategies are always evolving and changing along with the students. Students and technology are changing, so as we build years of experience in education our ideas must change as well."
Spanish		"That new generations are not worse than old generations, because people always say that and I hate it."

Table 5.15. Research Question Four Quotations: High School Science, Math and History Teachers

Subject Contracted to Teach	Years	Subject Taught/Quotation
Anatomy		"Novice teachers are eager to learn but often feel like they don't get the help they need from veteran teachers and are scared to ask because they don't want to bother the veteran."
Chemistry, Football, basketball	7	"Novice teacher would want veteran teachers to know about the upcoming changes that they heard about during their studies (in college trainings). The legislator makes big changes that affects novice and veteran teachers, and it is good to keep the veteran teachers who may be 'out of the loop' to know. Also, there may be new teaching strategies that have come up that veteran teachers do not know about, and new technology uses, that could keep them up to pace, that will help students succeed."

Subject Contracted to Teach	Years	Subject Taught/Quotation
Math	12	"He would want a veteran teacher to know that as a new teacher, he will take advice from them and is ok for them to help him, since they have many more years of experience."
History and Soccer Coach		"To be open to new ideas."
History		"I think they would want them to know that they have ideas too. It's important to feel heard with your team. Also, it is nice to get credit for things that are done really well. No one wants to feel invisible."

Table 5.16. Research Question Four Quotations: High School Vocational Education and Coach Teachers

Subject Contracted to Teach	Years	Subject Taught/Quotation
JROTC		"That novice teachers are new to teaching and do not know all the things necessary to be prepared for teaching careers. Also, know their teaching subjects well enough to properly teach the students. Also, that novice teachers will make a lot of mistakes along their career path as teachers."
Career and Technical Coordinator	13	"She would like for veteran classroom teacher educators to know that the expectations of the first year for new teachers out of touch."
Soccer Coach and History Teacher		"To be open to new ideas."
Football and Basketball Coach, Chemistry Teacher	7	"Novice teachers would want veteran teachers to know about the upcoming changes that they heard about through their studies (in college trainings). The legislature makes big changes that affects novice and veteran teachers, and it is good to keep veteran teachers who may be 'out of the loop' to know. Also, there may be new teaching strategies that have come up that veteran teachers don't know about, and new technology uses, that could keep them up to pace, that will help students succeed."
Varsity Soccer Coach		"That I need to be able to ask a lot of questions and need a lot of support and for you to be patient."
Girls' Soccer Coach	16	"Veteran classroom teachers should remember how hard it was when they had no experience and be compassionate to the new teacher."

Analysis of the subgroups. Elementary teachers had four responses that reflected that novice classroom teacher would want veteran teachers to know the importance of available support and knowledge as indicated by four of the five respondents. ". . . questions they might have . . .," "Without veteran classroom teacher educators they wouldn't know as much things and with the help the lessons will flow-by smoothly,", and ". . . most educators need additional help. . ."

The English and Spanish teachers had patterns emerge in their five of their six replies that reflected the importance of veteran teachers being open to new ideas from the novice teachers' perspective. "Those who are freshest out of school have had access to the newest techniques and research." "That change is good." and ". . . as times change so does teaching."

The science and math teachers brought forth patterns in their responses of knowledge and support which is one of the major themes throughout the analysis of subgroups responses to the four research questions. "Novice teachers are eager to learn but often feel like they don't get the help they need from veteran teachers and are scared to ask because they don't want to bother the veteran." ". . . . its ok to help him since they have many more years of experience."

The responses of both history teachers were interpreted as open to new ideas concerning what novice teachers would want veteran teachers to know. "To be open to new ideas," ". . . that they have ideas too." Be patient and understanding was the pattern found in common with both vocational education teachers' responses. ". . . the expectations of the first year for new teachers is out of touch." Two of the four coaches indicated that open to new ideas was what novice teachers would want veteran teachers to know. In summary the analysis of subgroup responses concerning what novice teachers would want veteran teachers to know revealed the importance of available support, knowledge, and be open to new ideas.

ANALYSIS

Elementary teachers had four responses that reflected that novice classroom teacher would want veteran teachers to know the importance of available support and knowledge as indicated by four of the five respondents. ". . . questions they might have. . . ", "Without veteran classroom teacher educators they wouldn't know as much things and with the help the lessons will flow-by smoothly", and ". . . most educators need additional help. . ."

The English and Spanish teachers had patterns emerge in their five of their six replies that reflected the importance of veteran teachers being open to new ideas from the novice teachers' perspective. "Those who are freshest out of school have had access to the newest techniques and research." "That change is good" and ". . . as times change so does teaching."

The science and math teachers brought forth patterns in their responses of knowledge and support which is one of the major themes throughout the analysis of subgroups responses to the four research questions. "Novice teachers are eager to learn but often feel like they don't get the help they need from veteran teachers and are scared to ask because they don't want to bother the veteran." ". . . . its ok to help him since they have many more years of experience."

The responses of both history teachers were interpreted as open to new ideas concerning what novice teachers would want veteran teachers to know. "To be open to new ideas.", ". . . that they have ideas too." Be patient and understanding was the pattern found in common with both vocational education teachers' responses. ". . . the expectations of the first year for new teachers is out of touch."

Two of the four coaches indicated that open to new ideas was what novice teachers would want veteran teachers to know. In summary the analysis of subgroup responses concerning what novice teachers would want veteran teachers to know revealed the importance of available support, knowledge, and to be open to new ideas.

CONCLUSIONS

This study's effort focused upon classroom teachers as associated teacher educators, with the specific research questions specifically revolving around classroom teacher expertise and understandings associated with teacher education programs of study and understandings focused upon novice classroom teacher needs. The research questions under focus were:

RQ 1: What would classroom teachers want university supervisors to know?
RQ 2: What would veteran classroom educators want novice classroom educators to know?
RQ 3: What are important qualities/components of teacher leaders that are necessary to support novice teachers?
RQ 4: What would novice classroom teachers want veteran classroom teacher educators to know?

In response to Research Question One, the classroom teachers emphasized the need for university-based faculty to remain informed about the realities of the clinical settings within school sites, to more appropriately meet the needs and understandings associated with teacher candidates and classroom-based teachers who are either associate teacher educators or site-based classroom teachers focused upon graduate studies. Also highlighted was the desire for university faculty to recognize the value of classroom teachers, toward connecting university coursework within the clinical experience so as to make such an exchange meaningful and effective.

In response to Research Question Two, veteran classroom teachers desired to emphasize understandings associated with classroom teaching for novice teachers, that "flexibility is critical," "teaching is not easy," "patience is key," that "learners need second chances to be successful," and perhaps vitally important is that "it's okay to feel stressed and to feel as if you're failing because it will become more comfortable as the novice teacher progresses in the professional classroom teacher career path."

Research Question Three highlights the recognition that novice teachers desire and require teacher leaders to be available and continuously supportive, with the additional understandings that teacher leaders must be able to share knowledge as well as reflect a high level of empathy toward the novice teacher's needs and levels of support necessary to be successful. The recognition of support is not only availability, sharing of knowledge, and a level of empathy toward the potential struggles and stresses acknowledged by novice teachers but also the sharing of resources, tools, skills, and strategies that the novice teacher may find to be useful as a just-in-time approach toward promoting the novice teacher's efforts.

Finally, Research Question Four reflected the needs of novice classroom teachers, with the desire to share what the novice would want the veteran classroom teacher educators to know. The overarching emphasis fell within the bounds of available support and availability of shared knowledge, and the desire of novice classroom teachers to be able to offer their ideas and the associated desire for veteran classroom teacher educators to be open to new concepts and creativity.

The novice classroom teachers acknowledge that there is so much to learn from veteran classroom teacher educators and the desire of the novice classroom teachers to learn this valuable information; while at the same time, there is a stated need that veteran classroom teachers remain open to new forms of practice from the novice teachers' perspective. As well, patience and understanding of the individual novice classroom teacher's needs is essential. Implications of this research reflect the need for teacher educators at all levels of practice to be accepting of the novice or veteran teacher where they are in the context of their professional development.

There is also the acknowledgment in the results of this study to authentically recognize professional development in the contexts of the learning communities as professional development environments and the individual teacher's further learning to teach objectives. Recognition of and advanced practice in the aforementioned principles further promotes teacher effectiveness when combined with a very real level of safety and comfort in offering, requesting, and accepting assistance and support in an open and welcoming community of practice.

REFERENCES

Association of Teacher Educators (ATE). (n.d.). *Standards for Teacher Educators*. Retrieved from http://www.ate1.org/pubs/uploads/tchredstds0308.pdf

Stake, R.E. (1995). The art of case study research. Thousand Oaks, CA: Sage.

Stake, R.E. (2005). Qualitative case studies. In N. K. Denzin & Y. S. Lincoln (Eds.), *The Sage handbook of qualitative research* (3rd ed., pp. 443–466). Thousand Oaks, CA: Sage.

Wenger, E. (1998). *Communities of practice: Learning, meaning, and identity*. Cambridge, MA: Harvard University Press.

Wenger, E. (2009). A social theory of learning. In K. Illeris (Ed.), *Contemporary theories of learning: Learning theorists . . . in their own words*. New York, NY: Routledge.

Wenger-Trayner, E., Fenton-O'Creevy, M., Hutchinson, S., Kubiak, C., & Wenger-Trayner, B. (2015). *Learning in landscapes of practice: Boundaries, identify, and knowledgeability in practice-based learning*. New York, NY: Routledge.

Afterword

Caroline M. Crawford and Sandra L. Hardy

Through this text, the Association of Teacher Educators (ATE) and the ATE Commission on Classroom Teachers as Associated Teacher Educators have attempted to engage in a vital discussion that revolves around the integral importance of teacher to teacher mentality in preparing and developing classroom teachers as associated teacher educators who engage in purposeful practice. The three separate yet related books of focus are designated as follows:

- *Redefining Teacher Preparation: Learning From Experience in Educator Development*
- *Dynamic Principles of Professional Development: Essential Elements of Effective Teacher Preparation*
- *Teacher to Teacher Mentality: Purposeful Practice in Teacher Education*

This book came into being, due to the vision of Nancy P. Gallavan, ATE president 2013–2014, who appointed this Commission and engaged Caroline M. Crawford as the Commission chairperson for a 3-year period.

Caroline articulated the Commission vision as the promotion of advocacy, equity, leadership, and professionalism for classroom teachers as associated teacher educators in all settings and supports quality education and collegial support for all learners at all levels. Further, the Commission mission was expressed as the promotion of quality teacher education through exemplary collaborations and collegial understandings that reflect the inherent importance of classroom teachers as associated teacher educators.

Based on the vision, mission, and goals of the Commission's efforts, this text is meant as a *state of the profession* as it revolves around the concept of teacher to teacher mentality of classroom teachers as associated teacher educators. This is an integrally important discussion to hold, and more important to bring forward research and scholarly efforts toward more fully understanding and articulating the reciprocity that inherently occurs in purposeful practice and within the deep-seated cooperative relationships transpiring within the realms of teacher education.

This relationship emerges between teacher preparation programs, to professional educators within the school sites, to the teacher candidate who works with professional educators throughout the transformational journey into a student teacher and then into a novice classroom teacher. Yet within these cooperative relationships one is becoming more aware of and recognizes the deeply appreciated works of the classroom teacher who takes on significant additional mentorship and collegial professional development efforts as an associated teacher educator.

This text and the related books are an initial attempt to highlight the current understandings, future directions, and associated scholarly efforts revolving around the important role of classroom teachers as associated teacher educators.

As a historical context toward framing the place of this text, and the other two sister publications, within the teacher education professional realm, classroom teachers have recognized their roles as a multifaceted approach toward the profession. Classroom teachers have been reinventing themselves, to fit within the Information Age and toward taking on differentiated roles that may be dependent upon differentiated learning theories of behaviorism, cognitivism, constructivism, and even connectivism. From *sage on the stage* to *facilitator* to *learner colleague* and beyond, dependent upon the instructional goals and instructional objectives.

A fun fact is that everyone has an opinion of the classroom teacher roles, including how classroom teachers should act, how classroom teachers should work, and even the different types of face-to-face, blended, and online learning environments in which classroom teachers currently find themselves engaged. Harrison and Killion (2007) stated that there are 10 roles for classroom teachers who are also actively engaged as teacher leaders, stated as being: "Resource Provider; Instructional Specialist; Curriculum Specialist; Classroom Supporter; Learning Facilitator; Mentor; School Leader; Data Coach; Catalyst for Change; and, Learner" (para. 3–21).

The Eton Institute also listed teacher roles that are inherently viable and useful within the 21st century: "The Controller; The Prompter; The Resource; The Assessor; The Organizer; The Participant; and, The Tutor" (para. 4–16). There are also innumerable researchers who desire to work out the beliefs, reasoning, and abilities of classroom teachers (Darling-Hammond, 2006; Kim, Kim, Lee, Spector, & DeMeester, 2013; Kleickmann et al., 2013; Nespor, 1987; Pajares, 1992; Putnam & Borko, 2000; Russell & Korthagen, 2013).

Yet after the researchers and scholars retreat to their offices with intriguing data sets and to work more closely with teacher candidates toward strengthening the candidate's understandings prior to the field-based experiences, a recognition arises. The depth of respect for classroom teachers as associated teacher educators undergirds a recognition of the integral and reciprocal relationships felt by all professional educators.

The identity, pedagogy, and self-efficacy embedded within the education profession is more fully realized throughout the teacher education profession due to the synchronous dance that occurs between teacher to teacher mentality and purposeful practice, pedagogy and andragogy, self-efficacy and mentorship that embraces modeling, and transformational journeys that directly impact one's shifting identity and sense of self no matter whether as a developing teacher educator or a burgeoning teacher leader.

References

Darling-Hammond, L. (2006). *Powerful teacher education: Lessons from exemplary programs*. San Francisco, CA: John Wiley & Sons.

Eton Institute (n.d.). *The 7 Roles of a Teacher in the 21st Century*. Retrieved from http://etoninstitute.com/blog/teacher-training/the-7-roles-of-a-teacher-in-the-21st-century

Harrison, C., & Killion, J. (2007, September). Ten roles for teacher leaders. *Educational Leadership, 65* (1), pp. 74–77. Retrieved from http://tinyurl.com/6xf4tpq

Kim, C., Kim, M.K., Lee, C., Spector, J.M., & DeMeester, K. (2013). Teacher beliefs and technology integration. *Teaching and Teacher Education, 29*, 76–85. Retrieved from http://media.dropr.com/pdf/WEvqzmQRL2n2yxgXHBVTGHGG0tLjpzc1.pdf

Kleickmann, T., Richter, D., Kunter, M., Elsner, J., Besser, M., Krauss, S., & Baumert, J. (2013). Teachers' content knowledge and pedagogical content knowledge the role of structural differences in teacher education. *Journal of Teacher Education, 64*(1), 90–106. doi: 10.1177/0022487112460398 Retrieved from http://tinyurl.com/j557qds

Nespor, J. (1987). The role of beliefs in the practice of teaching. *Journal of Curriculum Studies, 19*(4), 317–328. Retrieved from http://files.eric.ed.gov/fulltext/ED270446.pdf

Pajares, M.F. (1992). Teachers' beliefs and educational research: Cleaning up a messy construct. *Review of educational research, 62*(3), 307–332. Retrieved from http://media.dropr.com/pdf/9gnziXcoKpR4NEygcZferbvB3HonvxCa.pdf

Putnam, R.T., & Borko, H. (2000). What do new views of knowledge and thinking have to say about research on teacher learning? *Educational Researcher, 29*(1), 4–15. Retrieved from http://edu312spring13.pbworks.com/w/file/fetch/64649998/Borko%26Putnam.pdf

Russell, T., & Korthagen, F. (2013). *Teachers who teach teachers: Reflections on teacher education*. Oxfordshire: Routledge.

About the Editors

Caroline M. Crawford is an associate professor of instructional technology at the University of Houston-Clear Lake in Houston, Texas. She earned her doctoral degree in 1998, with specialization areas in instructional technology and curriculum theory, and began her tenure at the University of Houston-Clear Lake (UHCL) the same year. She is also a contributing faculty member in the Walden University Richard W. Riley College of Education and Leadership's Higher Education and Adult Learning doctoral program.

Her main areas of interest focus upon communities of learning, including communities of practice and learning in landscapes of practice, and the appropriate and successful integration of technologies into the learning environment; the learning environment may be envisioned as face-to-face, blended, and online environments, as well as microlearning deliverables.

Sandra L. Hardy, Ph.D., is an active researcher, board member, and former special education teacher. She served as teacher-induction consultant and coordinator of the after-school tutoring programs for students at risk. Dr. Hardy taught G.E.D. courses and served as adjunct faculty in the graduate program for teachers and administrators where she taught advanced educational psychology. She serves as vice president to the board of the Science Center and is very active in animal rescue efforts.

Dr. Hardy is a long-time member of the Association of Teacher Educators, and continues to be involved with the organization's efforts to support teachers and administrators locally, statewide, nationally, and internationally at all levels and stages of their professional development continuum. Sandra's research interests include induction, learning communities of practice, and professional development involving professional development organizations, P-12, and higher education, respectively.

About the Contributors

Billi L. Bromer, is an associate professor in the College of Education at Brenau University and the coordinator of Teacher Education at the university's regional campus in Augusta, Georgia. She is an active member of the state and regional chapters of ATE as well as the national association. She is a founding ATE Clinical Fellow and a member of the Commission on Classroom Teachers as Associated Teacher Educators.

Prior to becoming a teacher educator, Dr. Bromer was an early childhood special educator, providing collaborative consultation to teachers in Head Start, Georgia's Pre-K program, and other early education settings. During that time, she also served on the Georgia Department of Education State Advisory Panel for Special Education. Dr. Bromer was recently appointed as an NAEYC/CAEP Specialized Professional Association (SPA) reviewer and is firmly committed to the merits of collaboration among and between K-12 teachers and educator preparation programs.

Janine S. Davis is an assistant professor at the University of Mary Washington, where she teaches courses in action research, instructional design and assessment, teaching of English and theater arts, and a Freshman Seminar on persona and identity development as seen in interdisciplinary works. The ways that pre-service teachers develop and present personae and identities, whether in person or online, is the focus of her research. Social media, memoir, action research, and oral history figure prominently in her courses and her work, and her students' work within these formats informs her research.

Victoria B. Fantozzi is an associate professor of early childhood and childhood of education and chair of the Department of Curriculum and Instruction at Manhattanville College. At Mahattanville College she teaches courses in early literacy, foundations of early childhood education, action research, and social studies education. Her work on teacher education focuses on the perceptions, communication, and construction of narratives in student teaching.

Dr. Fantozzi also studies the intersection of literacy, technology, and play in the preschool classroom. She is currently working with a local preschool examining the ways a tablet can support storytelling and emergent literacy in a 3–4-year-old play-based classroom. Finally, Dr. Fantozzi writes about curriculum history.

Nancy P. Gallavan, Ph.D., is a professor of teacher education in the Department of Teaching and Learning at the University of Central Arkansas, a past president and distinguished member of the Association of Teacher Educators (ATE) and a Kappa Delta Pi (KDP) Eleanor Roosevelt Legacy Chapter inaugural member. With expertise in K-12 education, classroom assessments, curriculum development, cultural competence, social studies education, and teacher self-efficacy, Nancy is active member of American Educational Research Association (AERA), Association of Teacher Educators (ATE), Kappa Delta Pi (KDP), National Association for Multicultural Education (NAME), and the National Council for Social Studies (NCSS).

Contributing to more than 120 publications, Nancy has authored or coauthored *Secrets to Success for Elementary School Teachers*, *Secrets to Success for Social Studies Teachers*, *Navigating Cultural Competence: A Compass for Teachers, and Developing Performance Based Assessments* with Corwin Press, edited *Annual Editions: Multicultural Education*, editions 15, 16, and 17 with McGraw-Hill, and co-edited ATE Yearbooks XIX–XXVI.

Greg Gierhart is earning his doctorate from Southern Illinois University-Carbondale, with the specializations in mathematics education and science education through the curriculum and instructional doctoral program of study. Currently he is a lecturer in the Department of Early Childhood and Elementary Education at Murray State University in Murray, Kentucky, USA. He holds Kentucky Provisional Certificate licensure in grades 5–8, with a K-4 endorsement, in the mathematics, science, and Spanish teaching areas of specialization.

Meagan Musselman is an associate professor of education at Murray State University in Murray, Kentucky, USA. Before working at the university level, she taught middle-school math and science and obtained National Board Certification. She is the program coordinator for the Teacher Leader graduate program.

Lynn Gannon Patterson is an associate professor in elementary school education at Murray State University. She teaches math methods for elementary preservice teachers. At the graduate level she teaches integrating mathematics in the curriculum and classroom management classes. Additionally she is a National Board Certified Teacher, a Presidential Awardee in Elementary Mathematics, served as an elementary principal, and taught elementary school for many years. Her research interests include preparing preservice and inservice teachers to effectively teach mathematics through grant projects, problem solving in mathematics, differentiated instruction, and increasing student engagement in learning.

www.ingramcontent.com/pod-product-compliance
Lightning Source LLC
Chambersburg PA
CBHW030115010526
44116CB00005B/261